Hercules

Hercules

A Heroic Life

ALASTAIR BLANSHARD

Granta Books
London

Granta Publications, 2/3 Hanover Yard, Noel Road, London N1 8BE

First published in Great Britain by Granta Books 2005

A CIP catalogue record for this book is available
from the British Library.

1 3 5 7 9 10 8 6 4 2

ISBN-13: 978-1-8607-653-2
ISBN-10: 1-86207-653-7

Typeset by M Rules
Printed and bound in Great Britain by
Mackays of Chatham plc, Chatham Kent

To James, for none of the obvious reasons

Contents

Contents

Acknowledgements

Numerous debts were accumulated in the writing of this book. I am extremely grateful for the assistance and friendship provided by Anna Bonifazi and her family, Lucy Grig, Vicki Jennings, Ray Laurence, Polly Low, Paul Millett, Kathleen Riley, Kim Shahabudin, Amy Smith, Tracey Sowerby, Tiffany Stern, Peter Stewart and Peter Wilson. All of them helped, either wittingly or unwittingly, at various important stages in writing this work. My mother's talent for Greek has been a surprise and delight. Finally, if I have learnt anything about how to analyse antiquity and the footprints it leaves, it is only through the patience of two exceptional teachers: Suzanne Dixon and Paul Cartledge. The debt I owe them can never be repaid.

Introduction

The crowd that gathered in Paris to celebrate the Revolutionary Festival of the Unity and Indivisibility of the Republic in August 1793 was treated to quite a spectacle. The people were certainly in need of a treat. France, at this time, was at war with Austria, Spain, the United Kingdom, Naples and the Dutch Republic. Military disasters had forced French forces to retreat from Belgium. The summer had seen numerous uprisings in the west and south. Food was short and, despite official attempts to restrain them, grain prices were high.

Part pilgrimage, part history lesson, the festival aimed to offer the beleaguered citizens a vision of the new order established by the overthrow of the monarchy. In this it was typical of the series of festivals staged throughout the Revolutionary period. These events were designed to be educative as well as enjoyable. Centred around significant republican events or virtues, they helped through a series of impressive tableaux to give the people a sense of what it meant to be a citizen of the new Republic. So, for example, at the Festival of Unity, the crowd found, on the site of the hated Bastille, a giant Egyptian-style statue of the goddess Nature whose breasts shot great spurts of the 'milk of Regeneration' (actually water) into the air. A triumphal arch had been erected on the Boulevard Poissonière to commemorate the march upon Versailles in October 1789 that led to the king's capture and removal to Paris. At the Place de la Révolution a giant statue of Liberty now stood on a pedestal until recently occupied by a statue of Louis XV.

Yet, as they passed by and marvelled at these sights, nothing could prepare the crowd for the vision they encountered as they approached Les Invalides, the extraordinary complex of buildings built by Louis XIV as a hospital for soldiers and a traditional site of military parades and performances. Here was the centrepiece of the celebrations. Raised on a great mound of earth stood a colossus – a statue of Hercules, twenty-four feet high, gazing out triumphantly over the city. He was naked except for a 'cap of liberty' and a fig leaf to preserve his modesty. Additional support for the hero was provided by the fasces, the bundle of rods which symbolised a magistrate's power in the Roman Republic. At Hercules' feet was the vanquished hydra. Represented as half-woman and half-serpent, it lay sprawled flat out on its back unable to move, pinned to the ground by one of Hercules' feet. All fight had gone out of it. It clutched weakly at the fasces. In its other hand it held a mask, a symbol of its duplicity. There was a strong sense of immediacy about this piece. It seemed to be a victory that had only recently been won. Above his head, Hercules still held his club, ready to strike in case there was any life still left in his adversary. The crowd was being invited to witness the final moments in the destruction of dissent and discord.

Or so the President of the Convention explained. Standing in front of the statue, he provided an official explanation of the allegory to the gathering. He introduced the throng to

The Hercules of the French people destroys the hydra of discord in *Father Time Discovers Truth Trampling Feudalism*. Engraving, 1792.

a new symbol of the Republic – a hero who exemplified the strength, courage and power of the French people. The vanquished hydra represented the forces of counter-revolutionary revolt that had until recently been sweeping the country. A new epoch was dawning, he told them, one which would be an age of reason, justice and popular sovereignty. Previous symbols of the French people such as Marianne were to be brushed aside. This was to be an age of Hercules.

Such was the plan. However, like many such plans drawn up in the passionate delirium of year II of the new Revolutionary calendar, the elevation of Hercules to supreme symbol of the new Republic never came to pass. This was not for lack of influential backers. The artist Jacques-Louis David had masterminded the festival and the Hercules was his creation. It was a confident move on the part of a man at the height of his political powers. Elected to the Convention in the previous year, he had already served on the Committee of General Security and the Committee of Public Information. Four hundred and six warrants were endorsed with his name, including the execution orders for Louis XVI and Marie-Antoinette. Only two days before the festival he had presided over the dissolution of the Academy, an institution he had grown to detest. In putting forward Hercules as a symbol of the new republic, he had the full support of his close associate and leading Jacobin Maximilien Robespierre.

Initially Hercules must have seemed a good choice. His appeal for propaganda purposes was great. To a country in the grip of anticlericalism, this hero from classical myth could be offered as a replacement for Christian symbols. The adoption of Hercules represented the bold appropriation of a symbol that had been previously the preserve of the kings of France, who had frequently identified themselves with the hero. Like the palaces, artworks and other royal prerogatives, everything which had been previously reserved for the aristocracy was now being given to the people. Popular response was positive. The crowd at the Festival of Unity embraced their new symbol with fervour. It was equally popular with the Deputies. In November 1793 a decree was passed to erect on the Pont-Neuf a colossal statue, twice the size of the one in the festival, and to make it the symbol of the Republic on a new Great Seal of State. Ironically, the statue of Hercules was designed to replace a statue of Henri IV, the king who had done most to introduce the iconography of Hercules as a symbol of regal power into France.

However, even as these plans got under way, Hercules was proving a victim of his own success. One newspaper developed its own rival Hercules scheme. The editor of *Révolutions de Paris* suggested that statues of Hercules be erected in every city and hamlet in France, and because 'Homer called the kings of his time *mangeurs de peuples* [people-eaters], we will write on the figures . . . these words: *Le Peuple Mangeur de Rois* [The people, eater of kings].' To accompany the proposal there was an illustration showing a brutal bearded monster about to smash and devour a tiny crowned figure. Hercules began to appear in street theatre. For example, in Grenoble, two figures dressed as Hercules smashed mannequins of the Pope and the Nobility to popular acclaim and amusement. Hercules had become a side-show hoodlum. Things were starting to get out of hand.

Hercules was turning out to be an unreliable figure on which to build a new world. Rather than a symbol of dignified strength, he became increasingly associated with unrestrained violence. The massacres at La Force and La Salpêtrière were glossed by apologists as just the act of 'Hercules cleaning out the Augean stables'. The sabres and pikes that carved up traitors' bodies and held their heads aloft were likened to Hercules' own justice-dispensing club: brute force unresponsive to reason. Hercules all too easily became symbolic of the Terror. He became much harder to idealise as the Republic moved towards worshipping the cult of the rational and curbing the excesses of the sansculottes, the radical foot soldiers of the Republican revolution. He was turning into an embarrassment.

Hercules was still invited to the Festival of the Supreme Being in June 1794. Yet, already he was being upstaged by other Republican symbols. Engravings show him isolated on a column to the side of the main festivities, which centred around the Tree of Liberty. Hercules could not outlive the fall of Robespierre and the disgrace of David. In 1795 plans for the colossus were scrapped and the question of the design for the Great Seal was reopened. Hercules survived on coins, mainly through inertia, until 1798 when the Council of the Ancients, the upper house of the Revolutionary parliament, endorsed the removal of a figure described as 'an allegory whose conception and execution were not fortunate'.

This episode from French history illustrates a number of themes that I wish to explore here. This book is a history of ideas. It examines the ways in which Hercules and stories about him have been used and abused by different peoples and in different places. It is a study of myth in action. This French story of appropriation, its success and failure, could be retold using examples from many different periods of history right up to and including the present day. (The book concludes with a discussion of the most recent cinematic reworkings of the Hercules story.) What they demonstrate is that we have not become any cleverer at avoiding the pitfalls in our use of this character. Only by turning him into the most generic of superheroes can we produce something suitable 'for the whole family'. Even then, the old dangerous Hercules threatens to break through.

The myths about Hercules have exercised a fascination for Western culture ever since the time of the Ancient Greeks. It is no accident that the adjective for describing the most gigantic, excessive, prodigious things that we can comprehend is 'Herculean'. Hercules stands at the boundaries of our imagination. Despite this, or perhaps because of it, there has been no end of candidates willing to cast themselves as the 'new Hercules'. Of course, such claims require a certain amount of self-belief. However, this hasn't stopped many of history's greatest egoists, Alexander the Great, Marc Antony, the Roman emperor Commodus, Charlemagne, Cardinal Richelieu, Napoleon and Mussolini from attempting to claim his lion skin. The surprising thing is that each time this feat is attempted it more often than not ends in disaster. Marc Antony was dismissed as sharing only the flaws of his adopted hero. Mussolini was ridiculed by other European leaders for looking like a 'side-show strongman' in his propaganda. The Hercules myth turns out to be very hard to control. Hercules has too many dark sides. He is a drunk, a rapist, a transvestite, as well as a hero. He is often more than you can handle.

This book attempts to provide a taste of the wide range of ideas, opinions and attitudes that Hercules has embodied or endorsed. He has stood as the model of masculinity against which all men should measure themselves. He has also represented men at their most flawed and lowest ebb. He has been an inspiration as much to philosophers as to movie stars. A demi-god, he has helped us to understand the nature of divinity as well as mortal existence. Hercules puts great meaty flesh on to the rather thin concept of a hero. Traditionally, a hero for the Greeks was just somebody who received worship. Like modern 'trash celebrities', he, and occasionally even she, did not need to be virtuous, just famous. Over time, this idea has changed as morality has become increasingly bound into the fibre of the hero's being. Hercules 'the defender against evil' was integral in this transition. He has become the quintessential hero, the barometer by which we measure the meaning of the term. As each age has renegotiated its notion of the hero, Hercules has been there to mark that change. Stories about Hercules do far more than just recount amazing exploits, they take us into the heart of the culture that celebrates them. Through analysing some key images of the hero, I hope to elucidate some of the principal features of the societies that have adopted him as one of their own. Although reputedly dim-witted, Hercules turns out to be very good 'to think with'.

Introduction

The structure of the book follows Hercules' life: it begins with his birth in Thebes and ends with his death on a burning pyre on Mount Oeta in northern Greece. In between these two events we witness his growth as a young man, his tragic first marriage which ends with him murdering his wife and children in a rage, his performance of the twelve labours as a penance, and his wild adventurous life once released from the burden of his crimes.

In choosing to present the story of Hercules biographically, this work joins a long tradition. The father of modern biography, Plutarch, wrote a life of Hercules, now sadly lost. Our two best sources for his life, the mythographers Apollodorus and Diodorus Siculus, arranged their accounts of Hercules' exploits biographically. Biography attempts to make the world understandable. It is our response to chaos. Through telling the story of a life, we put events in order, see connections, understand causes and resolve apparent contradictions. Given the wide variety of myths that circulated about Hercules, the biographical urge is hard to resist.

Obviously, in choosing to write a 'biography' of Hercules, one needs to make choices. Almost every story in this book has a variant. Every statement should be qualified. There is even disagreement over the 'correct' order of the labours. If the central facet of Hercules' life cannot be agreed upon, what hope is there for consensus about the rest? I have not attempted in this book to provide a complete catalogue of all the Hercules myths. It would be beyond the scope of a slim volume like this one, nor would it be particularly helpful. It is too easy to get lost in the details and lose track of the ideas. For those who wish to explore the mythological tradition further, I hope the notes at the end will act as a useful guide.

A Note on Names

Greece and Rome often used different names for the same gods, goddesses and heroes (e.g. Heracles/Hercules, Zeus/ Jupiter, Hera/Juno, Athena/Minerva, Hermes/Mercury). For the sake of convenience, I have used the Roman Hercules throughout the text unless quoting directly from a Greek source. In other cases, I have used names appropriate to the origins of the material under discussion. Greek and Roman alternative names are noted in the text. Greek names have tended to be Romanised.

The Genealogy of Hercules

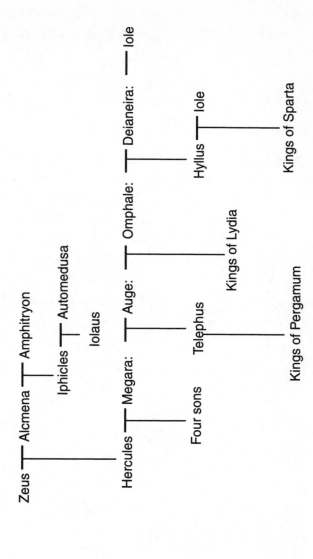

Map of the Mediterranean.

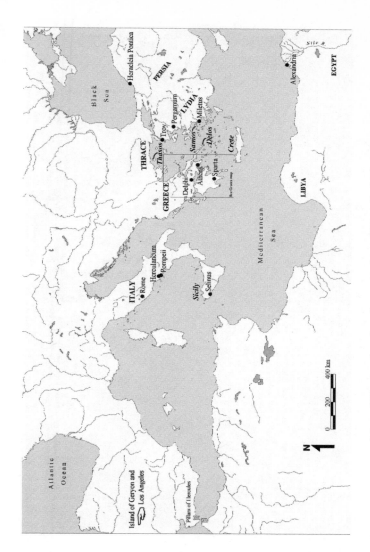

Map of Greece showing the main sites of Hercules' adventures.

CHAPTER ONE

Birth

Sometimes it is horrible to be right. The Roman ency-
clopaedist Pliny used to ridicule people for decorating their
walls with elaborate and expensive paintings. How, he won-
dered, would it be possible for their owners to rescue such
costly investments in the event of fire? Pliny was, of course,
correct, but the thousands of visitors to Pompeii each year
are glad that almost nobody seems to have heeded his advice.
Out of the ashes of the volcanic eruption that destroyed this
town in AD 79, archaeologists have unearthed hundreds of
examples of wall-paintings. Their bright colours evoke the
sumptuous decoration that adorned the houses of the
wealthy (and even not-so-wealthy) in this cosmopolitan
centre. The paintings depict a variety of scenes. Here we find
fantastic architectural vistas jostling with lush paradise

gardens, theatrical stage-sets and, most prized of all, vignettes from the lives of gods and heroes. This story of the life of Hercules begins with one of these paintings.

Hercules Strangling the Serpents as a Child. Wall-painting, House of the Vettii in Pompeii. After AD 62.

It is found in one of the houses most popular with modern visitors, the House of the Vettii. Located in the northwest of Pompeii, the house seems to have belonged to two brothers, Aulus Vettius Restitutus and Aulus Vettius Conviva. Until hot ash and pumice rained down upon them, fate had been kind to this pair. Ex-slaves, they had managed to acquire substantial wealth and high social position. Aulus Vettius Conviva had been made a priest of the imperial cult, one of the highest offices that could ordinarily be attained by a freedman. Perhaps as a consequence, they were not reticent about showing off their good fortune. The destruction caused by a small earthquake in AD 62 gave them the opportunity to renovate and handsomely redecorate their residence in the latest style and fashion. It is these paintings that attract so many visitors today. From the well-endowed Priapus weighing his member in the doorway to the pornographic scenes in the cook's bedroom to the scores of amusing cupids hard at work in the main reception room, these paintings entertain, inform and stimulate us just as much as their ancient audience.

Hercules can be found in one of a pair of reception rooms that flank the entrance from the atrium to the garden courtyard. As you enter the room, you see him on the left. It is a scene familiar from myth: Hercules the babe wrestles with the snakes sent to kill him. Joining us in watching this conflict, we find a number of other spectators. On the far right is Hercules' mother Alcmena. Next to her sits her husband, Amphitryon. Jupiter (Gk. Zeus), the true father of Hercules, is represented by his totem bird, the eagle, perched overlooking the scene. On the left we have a shocked slave – ubiquitous, anonymous and useful for balancing up the composition. It is a pretty conventional scene. It may even be a copy of a now lost masterpiece of classical Greek art, the equivalent of having the Mona Lisa on your wallpaper, and possibly just as kitsch. Even in a culture that did not place as high a premium on originals as the modern art-market, the Vettii were opening themselves up to sneers that, no matter how well they were doing, they weren't in the league of affording original painted panels. Still, it probably would have impressed their neighbours. Similar imitations of paintings are common and depictions of Hercules are popular throughout Pompeii. Over seventy-eight have already been catalogued. As one of the mythological founders of the city, there is clearly affection for him in the area. Earlier examples of the same scene have been found in houses in the city and nearby Herculaneum. There do not seem to have been too many risks in choosing this composition. Poets had already polished the scene up, and established it as a fit subject for aristocratic audiences. Approximately five hundred and fifty years earlier Pindar was already using the story to butter up a Sicilian autocrat, comparing Hercules' childhood adventures with this parvenu's achievement on the racetrack. In third-century BC Alexandria, Theocritus was offering lines on the subject for the enjoyment of the court of King Ptolemy Philadelphus. This was the company that the Vettii were hoping to join.

This scene is where depictions of the life of Hercules usually start: Hercules the demi-god is revealed to the mortal world. It is the first hint that somebody special has arrived. A number of guidebooks to the site even wrongly describe this as the first of Hercules' labours. Basking in the glow of Hercules' tremendous success (and so young!), it is easy to forget the rocky road that has brought us to this point. Most artistic depictions of the life of Hercules certainly do. Like the visual narratives for the life of Christ, depictions of the mechanics of Hercules' birth are hard to find. In choosing to focus on the moment when Hercules is revealed rather than created, we manage to erase some colourful moments from the story. So let us leave this wall-painting for the moment and see what it leaves out.

Part of the problem with the events prior to the birth of Hercules is knowing whether we are supposed to laugh or cry. We are not alone. The Ancients did not know either. The same sequence of events could equally be played as a comedy or a tragedy. The act of conception is not the problem. For once, we are spared the violent rapes that often accompany Jupiter's desire. Unlike previous conquests, Hercules' mother does not put up a fight. Instead, Jupiter tricks her into sex by appearing disguised as her fiancé, Amphitryon, returning from war.

In doing so, Jupiter strikes at the moment when things are finally starting to go right for this couple. He steals away a change in their fortune. Their bad luck had begun when Alcmena's brothers were killed defending themselves against a band of marauders, the Teleboans. Then, when her father, the king of Tiryns, a city on the Argive plain in the Peloponnese, had been organising an expedition to avenge their deaths, a club thrown by Amphitryon (either in anger or defence, the accounts vary) killed the king instantly. Exiled from his homeland for this killing, Amphitryon sought shelter and purification in the city of Thebes in central Greece.

He was joined by Alcmena who, deprived of male relatives, urged Amphitryon to avenge her brothers' deaths and refused to marry him until this act had been carried out. Indeed, it is this task that Amphitryon is carrying out when Jupiter arrives to sleep with Alcmena. It is only when the real Amphitryon returns that the deceit is discovered. By this time, Alcmena is already carrying Jupiter's child, Hercules. That same night intercourse with Amphitryon produces Hercules' mortal twin brother, Iphicles.

The Greek dramatist Euripides thought this was all pretty tragic stuff. His play *Alcmene* now survives only in fragments, but there is enough of it for us to reconstruct the general outline of the plot. Amphitryon, returning home and discovering that his wife has been having sex with another man, is driven mad with jealousy. He tries to kill her and when she escapes and seeks sanctuary at an altar, he piles wood up around it and sets it ablaze. Only the intervention of Zeus, who sends a thunderstorm to douse the flames, can bring him to his senses. Zeus effects a reconciliation between the couple by explaining that it was only when he was disguised as Amphitryon that he was able to seduce Alcmene. With a bit of nimble argumentation this act of adultery becomes an act of love and devotion. The play was clearly a hit. It enjoyed a number of revivals, and versions were performed throughout the Greek and Roman worlds.

Euripides' exploration of the life of Hercules' parents is the best-preserved of the tragedies that recount their lives. We know that most of the other major Greek tragedians also turned their hands to producing versions for the stage. Unfortunately, often nothing more than the titles of their works survives. Yet the atmosphere they evoked is clear. The conception of Hercules took place amid a maelstrom of passion, murder, revenge and deceit. On the face of it, there isn't much fun here.

It took the skill of the Roman comedian Plautus to see the humorous side. Indeed, this is the only mythological story that he seems to have found funny. Admittedly he was not the first to play up the elements of farce in the story. He most likely adapted a Greek original to create his *Amphitruo*. However, his play was no slavish imitation. In adapting this Greek play for the Roman stage, Plautus produced one of the original comedies of errors ('I'm Amphitryon'; 'No, *I'm* Amphitryon'). Shakespeare saw its value; his *Comedy of Errors* adopts just such a comic doubling.

Plautus' comedy represents a turning point. Throughout the classical world audiences had been accustomed to watching the actions of Amphitryon and Alcmena and feeling pity. Plautus admits in the prologue that he is offering up something unusual, a play that challenges conventional expectations. After him, comedy is the major vehicle for representing the story of Hercules' conception. The tragic elements are forgotten. Plautus' audience had recently been wowed by a revival of Euripides' *Alcmene*. Now they can only think of the conception of Hercules and laugh. This is how he tells the story.

The fun starts with a prologue by the god Mercury (Gk. Hermes) who sets the scene and explains that while

Hercules

Amphitryon is away fighting the Teleboans, Jupiter has decided to seize the opportunity to have sex with Alcmena. Mercury has been stationed outside the house to keep watch to ensure the lovers are not disturbed. This duty is made more onerous by the fact that in order to maximise his pleasure Jupiter has ordered the night to be lengthened. It may be a one-night stand, but Jupiter is doing his best to make sure that it is no ordinary night. Into this scene wanders the slave Sosias who returns ahead of Amphitryon to announce his arrival after securing a victory over the Teleboans.

In order to avoid Sosias barging into the house, disturbing the lovers, and exposing Jupiter's deceit, Mercury changes himself into an identical copy of the slave. Confronted by his *Doppelgänger* Sosias is confused, frightened and eventually tricked into doubting his very existence. A comic beating just adds to his existential crisis. 'Something has become Nothing,' bewails the Sosias figure in a twelfth-century comic version, as one of the central premises of philosophy comes undone. Indeed, while Alcmena is deceived and Amphitryon cuckolded, it is hard not to feel that the real victim of this play is Sosias. Bewildered and sore, the slave returns to his master, his message undelivered.

However, Mercury has only stalled the inevitable march of Amphitryon on to the scene. When he does return, confusion reigns. He gets a cool reception from Alcmena who cannot understand why he is making such a big fuss about his arrival, given that he left only a few moments before. She begins to question whether this is some sort of cruel practical joke. For his part, Amphitryon starts to wonder about the faithfulness of his beloved while he has been away on campaign. A few harsh words are exchanged. However, before matters can turn to tragedy, Jupiter returns and sets matters to rights. The precise details are a little obscure as some lines towards the end of the play are missing. From surviving fragments we can conclude that the play climaxes with the birth of Hercules and his dispatch of the snakes: a scene similar to the one that we've already encountered in the House of the Vettii.

The success of Plautus' vision of events is difficult to overstate. It dominates the subsequent reception of this myth. When thinking of the conception of Hercules, it is hard to imagine it except in Plautus' terms. Part of the reason for the play's success must be the realisation that when it comes to analysing these events, a comic turn is the most critically devastating. It invites us to do some thinking about the myth and the issues it raises. Adultery, fidelity, identity and divinity are all skewered in the comic versions of the play. None of the characters escapes. The comic framework sets up a variety of pathways for exploring some of the most basic aspects of human relationships. Beneath this playfulness, comedy has allowed artists to ask a variety of serious questions.

The gods, Jupiter especially, are subjected to particular scrutiny through these events. Jupiter's decision to have sex with Alcmena in the disguise of her husband raises some interesting issues. First of all, is it rape? Certainly, in a court of law, Jupiter would have no defence: consent achieved by deceit is no consent at all. In remarkably similar cases, rapists pretending to be the husbands and boyfriends of victims have been routinely convicted by modern juries. Although Potiphar's wife has often been invoked by barristers to demonise rape complainants as bitter spurned lovers, so far nobody has tried the 'Amphitryon defence'. The courts have seen few problems in ruling that sex by deceit is rape. Should we follow them? How much of a victim should we make Alcmena? The extent to which we are prepared to find Jupiter guilty of rape is determined by our ideas about consent, violation and intent. Even if we accept that such issues were a non-question for the original audience – and it is worth pausing and thinking through the implications of this – we might like to consider the moment at which they do become alive. The story should make us ask questions about rape and the consequences of its historical specificity. Is it rape by the time of medieval adaptations? The Enlightenment? The twentieth century? At what point in the history of this tale should our conception of the actions of Jupiter alter? What needs to change to bring about this transformation?

Questions of rape inevitably lead to questions of power. In this case, we might wonder what these actions tell us about the potency of Jupiter. It is hardly the most impressive demonstration of his power that, in order to enjoy a few brief moments of passion, he has to skulk about in the guise of a mortal. Refusal often offends, but not even being prepared to ask in the first place smacks of insecurity. The pettiness of his actions comes through all too clearly in a

Greek vase-painting from southern Italy. It depicts a scene from a comedy, possibly the one on which Plautus' play is based. Here we see Zeus accompanied by Hermes placing a ladder under a window; above, we see a woman traditionally identified as Alcmena. Zeus has all the dignity and majesty of a burglar – Don Juan with borrowed sex appeal.

Zeus' fondness for disguise is a continual joke. John Dryden has Mercury ask Jupiter sarcastically at the start of his *Amphitruo* (first performed in 1690) whether this time he is planning to 'fornicate in the Shape of a Bull, or a Ram, or an Eagle, or a Swan'. Offenbach extends the joke in a rondo from his operetta *Orphée aux Enfers*. Here the goddess Diana (Gk. Artemis), assisted by a laughing chorus, ridicules the god for his tendency to seduce lovers in disguise. Alcmena heads a list of conquests that includes Leda and Ganymede. In fact, Offenbach is being too kind. The list of lovers that Zeus has raped while in disguise as an animal or other creature is much longer. Antiope, Asterie, Europa, Nemesis, and Persephone could have been added. Even Alexander the Great claimed that Zeus seduced his mother in the form of a snake. 'Why these metamorphoses? Are you so ugly that you daren't show yourself in your true form?' jibes Cupid in Offenbach's libretto.

In thinking about rape, we might also learn something about myth. Why do the gods in myth seem to be able to resist moral censure? Zeus often appears as morally culpable as a tidal wave. The ethics of this act seem more pressing in a Renaissance drama such as Lodovico Dolce's *Il Marito* (1545) which adopts Plautus' *Amphitruo* storyline, but excises the celestial characters and replaces them with scheming mortals and lewd dialogue. The lack of the supernatural encourages identification, but is this the only reason the sexual politics resonate more strongly? Of course, not every reader is prepared to let the gods get off without censure. Plato found the morality of the gods troubling and early Christians were only too happy to ridicule their pagan brothers for worshipping such immoral beings. Both Hercules and Zeus are singled out by Christian apologists for their sexual promiscuity. However, such denunciations always seem a little zealous and puritanical. They miss the mark. The gods claim to come from a world before history and beyond judgement. The reportage of myth, which lacks a vocabulary of censure, bolsters such claims. Drama, on the other hand, seeks to puncture this invulnerability and bring these characters down to earth.

An examination of comic successors to Plautus under-scores this point. Molière, for example, was only too happy to take the gods for a ride. In 1668, the 46-year-old French playwright staged his version of the *Amphitruo*. The play was a huge success, delighting the king, who saw its third per-formance. Voltaire records that when he saw the play at the age of eleven, he almost fell over with laughter. Over 363 performances are recorded down to 1715. Dryden produced his English version in 1690 with music by Purcell.

Molière updated Plautus for contemporary sensibilities. His gods were even more passionate libertines. The play opens with Night berating Mercury about using language inappropriate to a god. However, inappropriate language soon gives way to inappropriate behaviour as Mercury out-lines Jupiter's tryst with Amphitryon's wife. With comic irony, Mercury explains that it is only Jupiter's exalted status that allows him to get away with activities that would be condemned in the lower classes. The high and mighty have licence to indulge themselves as they please. Such is the lib-ertine's creed, and Jupiter, when he appears, is quite the libertine. He may have taken the form of a husband, but what he really wants to be is a lover. Romantic fancies gush out of his mouth every time he sees Alcmena. To the amuse-ment of the knowing audience he keeps professing to her how much he wishes that theirs was not an affair legiti-mated by marital bonds.

In this Molière lays the foundation for the later adapta-tion by Heinrich von Kleist. Jupiter as the true romantic struck a chord in nineteenth-century Germany. Kleist's *Amphitryon* (1807) pits a stale conventional husband against a passionate Jupiter. Jupiter's morals are questionable. He is ruthless with Alcmena's feelings. However, compared to the emotionally stilted Amphitryon, a tyrannical figure besotted with public opinion, Jupiter comes across as the romantic hero. Between these two is Alcmena. Portrayed as the ulti-mate innocent, she captivates Jupiter. However, throughout the play the audience is left to wonder whether she is as innocent as she appears. Jupiter continually drops hints that she refuses to pick up. How much self-deception has gone on here? Alcmena is assailed by doubts, yet her resolution not to succumb to the obvious conclusions smacks of self-interest and a desire to hide herself from potentially harmful truths. Deep down she wants the transformation of her husband into a passionate romantic to be real.

Kleist tackles a theme that runs through all workings of the Amphitryon/Alcmena story, namely the definition of adultery and its resolution. Once again we are confronted with the issue of the classification of the act that occurs between Alcmena and Jupiter. In all the stories Amphitryon alleges it was adultery. Most versions are concerned with bringing him round to rejecting this view. In exculpating Alcmena from the accusation of adultery, the plays make her state of mind the touchstone of fidelity.

Adultery is committed in the head, not in the body. The idea seems thoroughly modern. It was certainly not one that enjoyed an unquestioned supremacy in the ancient world. It does not take much effort to find views where questions of adultery end with the sexual penetration by a man who is not the husband of the woman. Scant interest is paid to what goes on in a woman's mind. Indeed, a nagging dissatisfaction with the psychological definition of adultery runs through the early Italian adaptations of Plautus' *Amphitryo*. Here we see cuckolded husbands not entirely resigned to their position. Horns turn out not to vanish at divine fiat. No matter how innocent your wife's actions, it is hardly any recompense for going down as mythology's most famous cuckold.

Ultimately, it is the fool Sosias in all these scenarios who is the most honest. There is no sense that he feels any better for knowing that the thrashing he received was at the hands of a god. The readiness of Amphitryon and Alcmena to accede to divine will is a little embarrassing. Kleist is certainly critical. He represents it as just a game of status. The reconciliation of Amphitryon and Alcmena is all about social standing. It is only a social climber such as Amphitryon who, in a crass bargain with Jupiter, will accept the glory of a famous son as a fit pay-off for the deception of himself and his wife. Provided his standing in the community is improved, Amphitryon seems happy to tolerate whatever the gods dish out.

Furthermore, it is worth remembering that this is not the end of suffering for these mortals. In fact, the suffering that Alcmena has endured is only a taste of the suffering that she will endure giving birth to Hercules. Greek myth has a fondness for difficult, painful and prolonged labours. Leto wandered all over Greece before she could convince the island of Delos to grant her a place to give birth to Apollo and Artemis. Similarly Alcmena's pregnancy is traumatic. It is here that we first get a taste of the vengeance that Juno (Gk. Hera) will seek for the adultery of her husband. She dispatches the goddess of childbirth to impede Alcmena's delivery. The goddess waits outside Alcmena's chamber with her hands clasped together performing an act of sympathetic magic – as long as her hands remain together no child will enter the world. Art spares us the scene of Alcmena in the throes of delivery. We do not see the sweat and the blood, or hear the screams, the prayers for release that never comes. Only the Roman poet Ovid seems interested in playing out the implications of this moment. In his *Metamorphoses*, he has Alcmena recall with horror ('My limbs go cold as I speak') the seven days and nights she lay tortured by this birth. She recounts in detail her wish for death and the pity of all who saw her agony. Indeed, without the quick thinking of a midwife, the first victim of Hercules would have been his mother. The midwife, recognising the goddess and realising that while her hands were clenched together Alcmena would never give birth, ran out of Alcmena's chamber shouting joyfully that Alcmena had finally delivered a child. Caught by surprise the goddess releases her hands and Hercules and his twin brother enter the world. (For this act of kindness, the midwife is turned into a weasel by the furious Juno.)

A difficult beginning, and things don't get immediately easier. Plautus' play ends where the painting in the House of the Vettii takes off. Hercules has barely any time to recover from the trauma of his birth before he's fighting monsters. Fortunately, the snakes sent to kill him are quickly dispatched. In this moment, Hercules both announces his arrival and identifies his trademark characteristic – his strength.

While all the children of the gods were strong, none matched Hercules. His unique strength is a sign that this is no 'ordinary' hero. The origins of Hercules' strength puzzled people in antiquity and a number of versions circulated to explain it. One argued that Hercules' strength derived from the exceptional length of his conception. If it takes one night of love-making to conceive a mortal child, what must be produced after Zeus has been at it for a night extended threefold? Sex here is more than a transfer of semen; it is a physical transfer of virility. As ancient medical writers pointed out, it is for this reason that men feel exhausted after sex. (It is difficult to tell whether their lack of discussion on the effect on women reflects more their chauvinism or the quality of the sex.)

The second explanation is tied to Hercules' immortality. Mercury (another version has Minerva (Gk. Athena) as the agent) realises that Hercules will never gain immortality like the other gods unless, like them, he has suckled at Juno's breast. While Juno sleeps he sneaks up to Mount Olympus and nestles Hercules on her breast. Hercules gets a chance to suck, but only briefly. He sucks too hard, biting Juno, who wakes up and throws the infant still suckling from her breast. The milk that her nipple expresses as the baby is ripped away forms the Milky Way. The cruelty of a stepmother and the voyeuristic pleasure of surreptitious lactation make this an irresistible scene. Not even Galileo's telescopic discovery about the composition of the Milky Way could dampen Tintoretto's or Ruben's enthusiasm for the artistic possibilities it presented. Napoleon liked the scene so much, he used it to decorate a dinner service he gave to Tsar Alexander I of Russia.

You would think that a scene like Hercules and the snakes could not fail to make an impact. Shakespeare knew otherwise. He recreated the scene in the closing spectacular of *Love's Labour's Lost*. Towards the end of the play, the audience is treated to a 'Parade of Worthies'. Its choreographer, the pompous Holophernes, conceives the pageant as an inspiring and edifying spectacle. In practice it proves to be a farce. His cast are a crew of fools. His 'Pompey' cannot even deliver his lines before wits in the audience heckle him off the stage. Casting proves a nightmare. To play Hercules, he is reduced to using the puniest and most diminutive figure in the troupe. In desperation, he tries to cast the boy as the *infant* Hercules. The audience is less than impressed with Holophernes' tableau.

> HOLOPHERNES: Great Hercules is presented by this
>   imp,
>   Whose club kill'd Cerberus, that three-headed
>   canis;
>   And when he was a babe, a child, a shrimp,
>   Thus did he strangle serpents in his manus.
>   Quoniam he seemeth in minority
>   Ergo I come with this apology.

As his production lurches towards disaster, Holophernes learns what a playwright always knows – the trick is not the subject matter, but the staging. Pompeii teaches us a similar lesson. In order to appreciate the painting of Hercules in the House of the Vettii fully, it needs to be examined in context.

It is remarkable what a difference surroundings can make. Let us compare two versions of Hercules and the snakes from two different houses in Pompeii. We have already seen Hercules as expensive wallpaper in the House of the Vettii. Now let us see him as a garden gnome. One of the features of the House of Decimus Octavius Quartio in Pompeii is a long artificial watercourse, a miniature version of the Nile. Along its 'banks' were placed a number of figurines designed to evoke the extravagance of riverfront estates. Here are all the typical fauna of such landscapes: deer, hounds, lions – and snakes. The Romans did not need Genesis to tell them that the most luxurious gardens always come with serpents. However, in this case, the passing viewer need have no concern as he takes his stroll along the water's edge. The serpents are already being dispatched by the infant Hercules transported to the scene for a spot of pest control. It seems to have been a popular conceit. There are a number of copies of such statuettes.

What these statuettes bring into relief is the sombreness of the House of the Vettii. There is little room for affectionate whimsy here. Before this demonstration of Hercules' divinity, Amphitryon and Alcmena had only a faint suspicion about what they had on their hands. Now they are starting to learn. The House of the Vettii tries to warn us that this may well prove a painful lesson for them. The iconographic programme of the paintings in the reception rooms of the House of the Vettii can be read in a number of different ways. We know that part of the enjoyment that the Romans derived from such decorative schema was the opportunity they provided for viewers to display their learning and culture by spotting allusions, adding context and creating connections between the works. Certainly this reception room and its twin on the opposite side of the entrance to the garden invite the viewer to undertake such activity. On a basic level all the paintings in this room share a unity of place. They all concern Thebes, just as all the paintings in the other reception room show myths connected with

Crete. However, the themes that connect the paintings in this room go beyond location. One of the issues that they address is the revelation of divinity. The picture they paint is not a pretty one.

The central panel on the wall facing you as you enter the room depicts the death of Pentheus. He kneels surrounded by maenads, the wild female followers of Dionysus, who are about to rend him limb from limb. One clutches a rock in her hand. She is captured in the moment just before she dashes out his brains. Another leaps from a rock to stick him with her ivy-garlanded spear; in doing so she deliberates places her weight on to his extended right leg. The joint will clearly snap. The scene is gruesome. The figure of Pentheus looks up, imploring his attackers for pity. He knows that he will get none from the gods. One god, in particular, he has offended – Dionysus.

In Greek myth, Dionysus and Heracles have a lot in common. Both are children produced by the adulterous phil-andering of Zeus. Both are hounded by a jealous Hera. In both cases Zeus appeared to their mothers in disguise. Indeed, Dionysus' mother, Semele, is an object lesson in why those dis-guises are important. Tricked by Hera into requesting Zeus to appear to her as he appeared to Hera, she finds herself con-fronted by the god in a chariot ablaze with lightning. Her mortal body cannot withstand such a conflagration and Semele is swiftly consumed by the radiance.

Out of the ashes Zeus retrieves the embryonic Dionysus and sews the god into his thigh. Here the god gestates until the moment when Zeus undoes the stitches and the baby

Dionysus is born. However, Hera is still not appeased, and she wreaks a terrible vengeance on Semele's sister, Ino, and her husband, Athamas, for attempting to raise the child. Both are turned mad. Athamas hunts down his son thinking him a deer and kills him, while Ino throws another of their children into a pot of boiling water and then drowns herself. Only Dionysus is saved by Zeus who spirits him off to Asia. It is upon Dionysus' return to mainland Greece as a new god demanding worship that he encounters Pentheus.

The story of their encounter is captured in its most dramatic form in the *Bacchae* of Euripides and almost all the later Latin and Greek accounts are derived from it. In the play, the young prince refuses to acknowledge that Dionysus is a god. Instead, Pentheus accuses him of being a charlatan who has tricked a number of feeble-minded women into following him. For this arrogance and refusal to acknowledge the god, Dionysus destroys everything the prince holds dear. His palace is devastated by an earthquake. His pride is stripped off him as Dionysus humiliates him by tricking him into wearing women's clothing to spy on the cavorting maenads. Finally his life is taken from him as his mother, driven to a frenzy by Dionysus, kills her own son with her bare hands thinking him a lion cub. It is this moment of death that is captured on the wall-painting.

The painting stands as a stark warning of the dangers when new gods arrive on the scene. We may be delighted to see Hercules kill the snakes, but, as the example of Pentheus warns us, we ought to be aware that these divinities can be demanding. The other painting in the room does little to reassure either. It depicts the death of Dirce. Once again we are dealing with the aftermath of one of Jupiter's adulterous unions. This time the victim is Antiope who was raped by Jupiter, according to Ovid, in the form of a satyr. Her family refused to believe her story; they imprisoned her and exposed her children to the elements. The chief tormenter of Antiope was her aunt Dirce. After a number of years, Antiope escaped and was reunited with her sons, Amphion and Zethus, who had been rescued by a passing shepherd.

Eventually this pair exact revenge on their mother's tormentors and force them to acknowledge the truth of their mother's story and the divinity of their parentage. Dirce is shown having her hair tied to a bull that will trample her to death. It is a ghastly and exotic finale. Again we have a pleading figure who will receive no mercy. The offspring of the gods are just as sadistic as their parents. The threat of violence menaces everybody in this picture. Amphion's triumph over Dirce will prove to be shortlived. He is doomed to a life of inconsolable grief. In the near future, he will see his children mown down by the arrows of Apollo and Artemis as his wife, Niobe, tries vainly to protect them. Sources disagree about his precise end. Some say that grief drove him mad and that he was killed ransacking one of Apollo's temples. Others say that, overcome by his loss, he stabbed himself to death.

The punishment of Dirce was a popular scene in Pompeii. Five other examples have been discovered. In nearby Herculaneum there are a further two. What makes this version stand out is not only its quality, but its context.

The other paintings in the room echo and amplify its themes. The painting of the punishment of Dirce directly alludes to the death of Pentheus by having Dirce dressed as a maenad (she had been about to perform a rite to Dionysus when she was seized by the sons of Antiope). The figures of one painting are inevitably caught up in the events of the other. The paintings seek to bind themselves together. The sexual conquests of Jupiter and its consequences unite all three paintings in this room. The recognition of the divine and the arrival of the heroic are placed in the foreground. Further these are issues that are not to be celebrated, but problematised.

These paintings might make us reflect on the painting of Hercules with a little more intensity. Hercules is clearly the winner here. Who is the loser? In the first place, it is the agent who sent the snakes. In the vast majority of our sources this act is attributed to Juno, maddened by jealousy. However, in one version the agent was Amphitryon desiring confirmation of his paternity. Suspecting that at least one of the children might not be his, he releases a snake into their beds to see how they react. The shrieks of Iphicles confirm his mortality. Hercules' heroism indicates that he is the divine cuckoo. There is no clue in the painting as to who is behind this attack on the slumbering children. Amphitryon remains enigmatic. We have a record of one other depiction of this scene in Pompeii. There, Amphitryon is alarmed by the attack and moves to intervene. Here he is contemplative. The shrieking is left to others. However we interpret it, in a room full of action, such contemplation stands out.

Hercules

Amphitryon's quizzical stillness reminds us that Hercules' seizure of centre-stage has important consequences for the rest of the household. If we think through the version that has Amphitryon releasing the snakes, we are brought to marvel at a father who would be so keen for proof of his children's paternity that he would be willing to risk their lives to confirm it. Was he happy or sad when he saw the infant begin to throttle the snake in its chubby fist? We cannot tell. We have to make up our own minds. The death of the snakes is the death of normality for the family of Hercules. The painting wants us to look forward. At the infant's feet lies a miniature club. The Hercules of legend is starting to form. We are supposed to be seeing things in microcosm. Matters are not going to rest here. In a number of versions, after Hercules has strangled the snakes, Amphitryon sends for the seer Tiresias to interpret these strange events. He confirms what we, the viewers, already suspect. Hercules is bound to a destiny of triumph and tragedy. We should prepare ourselves for quite a ride.

CHAPTER TWO

A Restless Youth

The rage of adolescents can have terrible consequences, as Hercules' music teacher learns to his cost. There are few more horrendous stories about teaching going spectacularly wrong than the one that concerns Hercules and his music tutor, Linus, the brother (or sometimes teacher) of Orpheus. Linus is a strange figure. He was a puzzle to the Greeks. Many accomplishments are attributed to him. He is the supposed inventor of the cithara, a multi-stringed instrument similar to the lyre, as well as the names and shapes of letters. Yet beyond this point the stories start to go awry. Linus turns out to be not so much a person as a talisman, a stock figure. He is the figure you introduce when somebody needs to die. Every story with Linus ends with his death. Death defines him, it is his distinctive feature. The historian

Hercules

Herodotus wrote that every culture has its Linus. Sometimes dogs devour him. At other times Apollo kills him for boasting that he was as good a singer as the god. One of the most popular versions of his death is to have him killed by Hercules, his music student. The young hero did not take to music lessons. Some traditions say his stubby fingers proved unable to cope with the complexity of the lyre. Others complain that his spirit was unmusical. Still others say that he was driven by jealousy of the superior skill of his brother. In any case, the criticism of Linus becomes too much, and one day when he physically chastises his pupil, Hercules rises up and strikes his music teacher dead.

It is a story that is supposed to teach us about teaching. The physical chastisement of students was always problematic in a culture where the teacher often occupied a much lower social position than his students. The sort of anxieties that the teacher–student relationship generated varied according to time and place. Sometimes sex was the issue, and laws were passed to prohibit the social hierarchy being upset by the sexual predations of low-class teachers. At other points, the Greeks and Romans worried about beatings, some states banning corporal punishment by slave teachers on freeborn children. In every case, the issue comes back to status. And what bigger status gap can there be than that between a teacher and the son of Zeus? The story of Hercules reminds teachers that when they chastise students physically they are taking their life in their hands.

It is also a story with greater ambitions. Through it we can speak about culture, its limits and its threats. Society binds itself to individuals through education. A number of lists circulate that catalogue Hercules' teachers. Although none of the lists agree, they all read like a *Who's Who* of Greek pedagogy. Everybody who was anybody was linked with the hero. From these various teachers, Hercules acquires all the martial skills required for his subsequent adventures. As befits the founder of the Olympic Games, chariot-driving, archery, javelin-throwing and wrestling all come easily to him. However, although Hercules readily masters physical skills, culture eludes him. In this respect, his education can be regarded as a failure. Traditionally, Greek education was composed of three elements – music, letters and gymnastics. Hercules falls at the first hurdle. He is doomed to be a permanent outsider.

Certainly this interest in the limits and threats to culture occupies an early fifth-century red-figure cup decorated by the Athenian painter Douris. As with every other Athenian vase-painter, we know almost nothing about this artist. He signed his name to a number of vases. Others are attributed to him on the basis of the tell-tale signs of an artist's style – the way he draws an ankle, the profile of a nose, the curve of the lines that make up the eye. In trying to recover Douris the only thing that we have to go on is his work.

What this work reveals is a mind that loved to cast a critical eye over one of the principal institutions of Greek life, the symposium. This is perhaps understandable. After all, this institution helped to provide his livelihood. Its performance required a large number of the vases and drinking cups that he produced (Douris was also a potter) and decorated. The symposium was the cornerstone of male social life.

These highly ritualised drinking parties were opportunities for display and competition. They were governed by elaborate rules about the amount of wine that could be consumed, the ratio of water that could be mixed with wine, the order in which the drinks would circulate and the topics of conversation that drink would generate. The most famous symposium from antiquity, so famous it even steals the name of the institution for itself, was Plato's *Symposium*. In many ways, this text gives a bad impression of the symposium. Certainly many symposia were happy to devote time to its central topic, love. However, as one might expect from Plato and Socrates, this symposium is like no other. In its high philosophical discussion, its denial of distractions such as music, song and dance, its general sobriety, it distinguishes itself from other symposia.

The main problem with Plato's *Symposium* is that you never feel that things might get out of control. Even when a group of drunken guests bursts in upon the action, order is quickly restored. This seems far removed from more normal drinking parties where the mixture of male ego, competition and alcohol meant that the potential for riot was always present. So ubiquitous were these outbreaks of disorder that a litigant in a court case tries to pass off his vicious assault on another member of the Athenian public as just the sort of thing that happens when young men get together – they drink, fight and break into brothels.

It is against just such activities and their consequences that the red-figured cup of Douris warns. On its inside we see a scene from a symposium. It is always worth paying attention to the inside of cups. These are the images that the painter wants you to see between draughts. Sometimes as you drain your cup you will see your reflection fade away to be replaced by a leering satyr. At other times you will be rewarded with some titillating pornography. In this case you are confronted with yourself. Or rather, yourself if you do not stop drinking. The scene shows a guest reclining on a couch at a symposium. He is attended by a flute boy, a potential object of desire. The guest clutches his brow, and throwing back his head he exclaims in letters that proceed from his mouth '*ou dunam' ou*' ('I am unable'). High-minded classicists have seen an allusion here to a poem by Theognis that begins similarly. Theognis' poem tells how, owing to drink, he is unable to sing. This may be right. Although, given the presence of the comely youth by his side, the painter may be pointing us in another direction.

The dangers of drink are also repeated on the outside of the vessel, although here the warning is not about incapacitation, but the potential of drink to promote violence. Here we see the young Hercules murdering his music teacher. His fellow students raise their arms in protest, but Hercules is immune to their cries. His face is grimly set. The uncontrollable, disproportionate rage that he feels is the rage of the drunken man. Hercules, famous in antiquity for the amount that he could drink, stands for us when we are in our cups. Pathetically, Linus raises his lyre in self-defence. We know that it will prove no use. His strings will soon be silenced. Once again there will be no more singing.

The death of Linus then is more than a child's natural

desire to kill their piano teacher writ large. It marks Hercules' break with civilised society. Heroes always stand on the outside. Their passions make them unsuitable members of a community. They cannot be assimilated, only propitiated. Greek culture was used to such figures. Someone once asked why the Athenians put up with the wild excesses of Alcibiades, a statesman and general who was the closest thing that the fifth century produced to a real hero. The reply: 'It is best not to raise a lion in your city, but if you do, treat him like one.' It is the same logic that underpins the treatment of the young Hercules.

This idea of Hercules as a threat to civilisation and order stands at odds with a few representations where he appears as a champion of culture. This is not just in the labours where his defeat of various monsters ensures the preservation of society. As we shall see, unless one adds a lot of gloss, Hercules makes a fairly thin culture hero in these adventures, his virtues being little more than a quick temper, a brutal disposition and a good knowledge of how to use his fists. Yet in some manifestations, Hercules is presented, cithara in hand, as a companion of the Muses. He even shared a temple with them in Rome, near the Circus of Flaminius.

There is a contradiction here, but one that perhaps we overstate. We misunderstand the Muses if we regard them as a group of gentle aesthetes. Passion flows through their veins. Songs of heroic rage are tunes that they happily sing. Their choice of Hercules as a companion reminds us that they liked a bit of rough. The Roman satirist Lucian knew that any wedding of Hercules and culture could not be a normal state of affairs. In one of his works he describes a barbaric cult of Hercules that worships him as a master of rhetoric and eloquence. Of course, it is eloquence with a Herculean twist. To symbolise his way with words they depict him dragging people by their ears with chains attached to a hook driven through his tongue. It takes Hercules to show us the implicit brutality in rhetoric. The funny thing is that Lucian's jokey, gruesome image got taken seriously. He located his cult, appropriately to his cosmopolitan mind, in the barbarous land of Gaul. This was enough for his so-called Gallic Hercules to become adopted by a number of French artists as a popular symbol of France.

Following the murder of his teacher, we see Hercules consigned to the wilderness. His father arranges for him to act as a cowherd in the hills around Thebes. A number of minor adventures are attributed to Hercules during this period. Their interest mainly lies in the way they presage later events. This is a common conceit in ancient biographies. People rarely developed; they just ended up performing the same actions on an ever-grander scale. So his first labour, the defeat of the Nemean lion, is foreshadowed by his defeat of the lion ravaging Mount Cithaeron. We sample Hercules' sexual excesses through his conquest of the fifty daughters of Thespius. In some versions, he does this all in a single night. In other versions, he was assisted by Thespius himself who, realising that Hercules provided good heroic stock, entertained the hero for fifty nights and substituted, without Hercules apparently noticing, a different daughter each night as a bed-companion: Hercules not so much as hero as stud bull.

However, this carousing and random adventuring needed to be checked. Some grander purpose was required. To make this life seem more constructive, it would be helpful if Hercules started making some commitments. Certainly, the philosophers seemed to think so. One of the most enduring parables from the life of Hercules is the so-called 'Choice of Hercules'. It first makes an appearance in literature in the *Memorabilia*. This work written by Xenophon, the exiled Athenian mercenary commander, keen huntsman and former student of Socrates, consists of a number of sections, some of which are Socratic dialogues similar in style and form to those found in the works of Plato. In one, Xenophon records a conversation between Socrates and his student Aristippus on the subject of how to raise children. Aristippus contends that there is no point in raising children to be leaders as the burdens of leadership seem to produce just as miserable a life for leaders as those endured by their followers. In fact, he argues, their suffering may be greater. Socrates responds by arguing that burdens accepted freely and for a noble purpose are less of a burden than those endured through necessity. Rather, the assumption of noble burdens elicits the praise and envy of all.

To illustrate his point, Socrates recounts an anecdote from a lecture by his friend, the diplomat and teacher of rhetoric Prodicus. Hercules, when he was approaching manhood, found himself confronted by two women. One claiming to be Virtue was tall, slender and wore a simple white robe. The other, Vice ('although my friends call me Happiness'), was shorter, plumper, wore full make-up and dressed provocatively. Each sought to woo Hercules and entice him towards a life of virtue or vice. Vice offered him the pleasures of the table, the bottle and the bedroom. With her Hercules could pass his life in comfort. In contrast, Virtue offered Hercules a life of toil and struggle. The only compensation that she can give him is undying fame. As the text breaks off, it is a bargain that we are left to assume the hero accepts.

The structural appeal of the story is clear. We find numerous variants circulating round the ancient Mediterranean and Near East. Local heroes are regularly substituted for Hercules. In Rome, Scipio has a similar dream. Egypt produces its own version. The image lingers in Western imagination. It has been appropriated as Christian allegory, political symbol and a metaphor for university education. Both Handel (HWV 69) and Bach (BWV 213) put the 'Choice of Hercules' to music. Artists such as Veronese, Poussin, Rubens and Ricci captured it in paint. It just missed out on being placed on the seal of the United States. John Adams was keen, and the allegory was agreed to be fitting. Unfortunately, the complexity of the design ultimately counted against it.

The anecdote has a dual focus. On the one hand, it is supposed to rescue the career of Hercules from being just a series of adventures. It introduces a purpose to his story. The temptation to find meaning in Hercules' adventures is a strong one. Diodorus Siculus even claims that Zeus slept with Alcmena only so he could conceive a hero to bring order to the world. Lust had nothing to do with it. Allegorical interpretations of the Hercules myth abound. Underneath every adventure lies a moral waiting to be discovered. The Hercules myth is ethics written in code.

On the other hand, this story is not about Hercules. It is about us. It loses its point unless we can place ourselves in Hercules' shoes. Unlike many of Hercules' labours where we can only fantasise about imitating the hero, the 'Choice of Hercules' is one that we can all make. Re-enacting the 'Choice of Hercules' even became an eighteenth-century pastime. A number of garden designs include a Temple of Virtue perched up on a hill. As walkers take their stroll they are confronted by numerous choices. Various grottos, ornaments and follies exist to distract them. The slothful can remain on the lower walks. In contrast, the energetic can take their exercise through a brisk walk up the hill to the Temple of Virtue. Here they would be rewarded not only with spectacular views, but often with a statue of Hercules smiling approvingly at their choice.

Making choices about the 'Choice of Hercules' reveals a lot about one's character. One of the most foolish must have been the decision made by Tony Blair's advisers not to allow him to be photographed in front of Carracci's *Hercules at the Crossroads* (1596–7) at the opening of the Royal Academy's 'Genius of Rome' exhibition because they were concerned that Hercules' genitals would hang just above the Prime Minister's head. As we shall see, there are many reasons why the Prime Minister might not want to be photographed in front of this painting; this is the least of them.

Annibale Carracci's painting is *the* iconic representation of this moment. The painting forms part of a commission to decorate the study of Cardinal Odoardo Farnese. Carracci's work at the Palazzo Farnese marks his transition from Bologna to Rome and cemented his reputation as one of the premier painters of the Baroque period. His paintings for the

Annibale Carracci, *Hercules at the Crossroads*. 1596–7.

study and long gallery have regularly been offered as rivals to the masterpieces of the Sistine Chapel. The painting is the central scene in a series of works that decorate the cardinal's study on the first floor of the palace. The iconographic programme for the room was most probably devised by the talented polymath and Farnese librarian Fulvio Orisini.

We should not be surprised that the designer chose the achievements of Hercules as the dominant motif for the room. The Farnese love of antiquity had already been demonstrated by Odoardo's great-uncle, the celebrated Cardinal Alessandro Farnese, whose collection of antiquities was one of the largest in Rome. Models for the ceiling can readily be found among the marbles in the collection and the room overlooks the courtyard where one of the most famous statues in the collection stood, the Farnese Hercules, a Roman copy of the masterpiece by Lysippus. Moreover, Hercules was a popular choice of subject among courtiers as he provided an extremely useful vehicle through which they could flatter patrons. Noble youths could be likened to a young Hercules about to start their life's journey. Already the precocious Odoardo (a cardinal at the age of seventeen) had been the subject of one such arrangement of verses. That Odoardo is the intended recipient of this image is indicated by the presence of Pegasus at the end of the path to virtue. The image of Pegasus on Parnassus had been used by Alessandro Farnese to signify his patronage of the literati. Pegasus personalises the message of the picture by holding out the example of Odoardo's great-uncle as the relative whom he should most imitate.

Yet, it would be a mistake to see the painting as just a piece of didactic flattery. Carracci is keen to tease out the moment of choice. Balancing on the edge between pleasure and vice is where the artist has chosen to place this Hercules. In an earlier fresco in the Palazzo Sampieri in Bologna, Carracci had depicted Hercules safely in the hands of Virtue. In contrast, here nothing is decided. The outcome remains uncertain. Vice with her lush vines and Hercules' lifelong fondness for wine might make us wonder who was the victor in this contest. Critics have been only too keen to point out the numerous times Hercules deviates from the path of virtue. One even playfully interpreted a Pompeian fresco as depicting Hercules being punished by Athena for his lack of resolve. Is the look that Hercules offers Virtue one of attraction or apology?

Complementary images underscore the importance of this moment. On either side of the painting are depictions showing what is at stake. The pendants to this painting are *Hercules Bearing the Globe* and *Hercules Resting from His Labours*. These are more than just snapshots from his life. They symbolise the two types of virtuous life, the contemplative and the active. In *Hercules Resting*, the hero is surrounded by the monsters he has vanquished; their corpses are testament to his boundless energy. In the companion picture Hercules is immobilised by the weight of the world on his shoulders. The painting alludes to a popular allegorical interpretation of the Hercules and Atlas story. According to this version, Atlas was an astronomer from whom Hercules learned the science of the heavens. It is the weight of scholarship that is keeping the hero still. Both these pictures demonstrate what will be lost if Hercules makes the wrong choice.

Hercules

The power of temptation is rife throughout the rest of the room. At one end, the scantily clad seductress Circe attempts to lure Ulysses into drinking a charmed potion. At the other end, Sirens sing their treacherous song attempting to draw sailors to their doom. Carracci is keen to point out that the 'Choice of Hercules' is not as easy as the Christian moralists who regularly appropriated this story would have it. Virtue alone is having a hard time of it. Only when she is joined by a poet promising everlasting fame does the balance seem to tip in her favour. Virtue will not be its own reward. In reminding the viewer that the 'Choice of Hercules' is just as much a choice about fame over pleasure, Carracci takes the story back to its pagan roots. The pursuit of undying glory, rather than any abstract notion of goodness, is what ultimately drives the story of Prodicus. It is the suggestion that claims of virtuous behaviour may equally be read as crass publicity-seeking that offers a better reason for politicians to run from this image than sterile classicising nudity.

Ultimately, whatever the motive or whatever decision Hercules makes, the simplicity of his choice is to be relished. As Cicero observed, the long-held appeal of this story rests on its fantasy. If only things were this simple and clear-cut. Sadly, it is rarely the case that our choices are this stark and the consequence this clear. If only steering a path between virtue and vice were just a matter of choosing the right partner. We never have it as easy as Hercules.

CHAPTER THREE

The Madness of Hercules

Hercules' adult life begins and ends with episodes of madness. It is his murder of his wife and children which starts him on his heroic journey, and the maddened agony of his death heralds his eventual apotheosis. Since antiquity, his rage has been famous. His madness was infectious. One theatre anecdote told about Julius Caesar recalls the time that he played Hercules on stage. Midway through the performance, Caesar became so overwhelmed by his character's fury that he killed one of the other actors and proceeded to swing the corpse around the stage, showering it with blood before being eventually restrained and brought back to his senses.

Such stories are always the most popular among the theatrical profession. Such was Caesar's fame that this anecdote about him even made its way into a defence of the acting profession offered when the theatre was under attack by the Puritans during the Renaissance. These tales provide a glimpse of the one thing that actors strive for, but can never achieve – the complete collapse of art and life. Yet, what is striking here is the implement used to pierce the veil of arti-fice. To lose yourself in the moment requires a madness as wild as Hercules'. The power of the Roman dictator proves no match for the power of the script. To further explore the power and potential of this passion, let us begin with a couple of pieces by the sculptor Antonio Canova that caused a stir in the nineteenth century.

It is hard to appreciate fully the passion that Canova's work elicited in his contemporary audience. At its height, his following had all the elements of a cult. In the late eigh-teenth and early nineteenth centuries, members of fashionable European society threw themselves at Canova in increasingly desperate bids to have their likeness captured in marble during their life, and to consign their bodies to his monuments after they died. He happily posed members of the aristocracy as modern-day cupids or, like King Ferdinand of the Two Sicilies, dressed them in drag as Pallas Athena. Tombs, sepulchres and mausoleums were among his most important commissions. Popes and royalty were interred beneath his overblown fantasies. His marbles redefined the notion of idealised beauty, and perpetuated the domination of classicism in Western aesthetics. Viewing his work, critics thought that the great age of classical sculpture had been reborn. To a world in the thrall of the recently arrived Elgin marbles, Canova seemed a talent to rival their supposed creator, Pheidias. His ability to unite Eros and Thanatos – Love and Death – makes Canova the ideal starting point for a discussion of these most painful and tragic episodes in the Hercules myth.

These episodes more than any other seem to have captivated Canova. His sketches of the labours never translated into finished work. The final moment of madness involves Hercules raging in pain as a shirt mistakenly impregnated with poison by his lover Deianeira clings to and burns his flesh. This is pain so terrible that even the heroic Hercules will not be able to bear it. Only his death in the cleansing flames of his funeral pyre can end it. In his rage, he picks up the page Lichas, who was sent bearing the fatal garments, and hurls him into the sea. It is this moment that Canova captures in one of his most celebrated works, *Hercules and Lichas* (1815). It is a tour de force of momentum and madness. Lichas clings desperately, but in vain, to an altar. His fingers seek to gain purchase in the mane of Hercules' lion skin. It will do him no good. And he knows it. His mouth is contorted in a scream. Hercules is a vision. He is fulcrum and force personified, a deadly catapult. He matches the violent terror of Lichas with grim determination. Through the sculpture's ghastly symmetry, we watch two victims act out their final moments on earth.

Less successful, but all the more interesting for that, are Canova's attempts to depict Hercules' first moment of madness. These encompass all the media in which he worked: he painted, sketched and made wax models of this scene. In the

Canova museum in his home town of Possagno, we find the final version, a plaster relief depicting this episode. It is grisly. The murdered bodies of Hercules' children surround the

Antonio Canova, *Hercules and Lichas*. 1815.

hero. The living have scattered in a futile search for safety. One child buries its face in the altar. Shielding its eyes and ears, it attempts to deaden its senses to the surrounding scene. At one end of the relief stands Hercules' wife, Megara. In one arm, she cradles his dead son. With her other hand, she reaches out. It is a gesture partly of supplication, partly to ward off the doom that she knows lies in the arrow that has just started its journey from Hercules' bow. In the distended, unreal arc of her frame, we can already sense the inevitability of its death–dealing thrust. We have caught the drama at the instant before its climax. Hercules' stepfather, Amphitryon, throws out his arms in a desperate attempt to avert disaster, and bring his son to his senses. However, the arrow has left the bow. We know it is already too late.

This scene offers a striking contrast to the image of Hercules that closed the last chapter. There, his position seemed to be one worth coveting. In his dispassionate weighing-up of the competing enticements of Virtue and Vice, Hercules was in control. Reason seemed to have triumphed over emotion. Hercules became the very model of the contemplative philosopher. The sequence of events that brought about this transformation is worth elaborating.

The metamorphosis of Hercules from the solitary figure standing at the crossroads of life into a juggernaut of domestic violence begins with his return to Thebes after his sexual excesses with the daughters of Thespius. Making his way back, he encountered some emissaries from Egrinus, a neighbouring king, to whom the Thebans owed an annual tribute of one hundred cattle, exacted from Thebes after a dispute over an injury done to Egrinus' father at a festival. Greek festivals were notorious for their drunken, raucous and often uncivilised behaviour – this one does not seem to have been an exception.

According to some versions, the father was killed; according to others, he was only injured. In any case, Thebes was held responsible and forced to pay compensation. It was to retrieve this tribute that Egrinus had sent his messengers.

The payment of tribute is something that heroes cannot abide. Theseus, for example, objected to the offering of seven youths and maidens to Minos. Substituting himself in the place of one of them, he set off a chain of events that involved the seduction of Ariadne, the slaying of the Minotaur, and his cunning escape from the labyrinth by means of a thread smuggled into the maze. Hercules' response to the demand for tribute was equally robust, if less swashbuckling. In place of the cunning of Theseus, we find straightforward thuggery. Hunting down the emissaries, Hercules cuts off their ears, noses and hands. These body parts he weaves into necklaces for the mutilated messengers, and then bids them return to Egrinus wearing this macabre jewellery as tribute. This deed was not quite as ingenious as Theseus' actions, but then one's heroism was not compromised by either trickery or assault. Heroes come in all shapes and sizes. They can be cunning like Odysseus with his hollow horse, or monsters like Achilles, who mutilated the body of Hector before the walls of Troy.

Egrinus' retaliation is immediate. He summons his forces and marches on Thebes. In battle he is opposed by Hercules who leads the youth of Thebes out against the invaders. Hercules and his band are successful. Egrinus is defeated, and the grateful king of Thebes awards his daughter Megara to Hercules. Everything so far seems to conform to a storyline that we know well. A boy from the wrong side of the tracks (a wild cowherd from a noble family fallen on hard times) defeats the villains, and wins the hand of the king's daughter. If this were a movie, then the music would well up at this point, and we would leave Hercules and Megara hand-in-hand gazing off into the distance. Indeed, this is precisely what Disney do in their animated version of the Hercules story. The final scene closes with Hercules and Meg(ara) wrapped in each other's arms, smiling blissfully while a troupe of Motown-inspired muses warble in the background.

Greek narratives dance to a different tune, one that prefers to couple rise with fall, success with disaster, pleasure with pain, and sanity with madness. For no sooner have Hercules and Megara settled down and started to raise a family, than ever-jealous Hera sends a divine madness on to Hercules. Enraged, he smashes up his home and kills his wife and children. Everything that made his life worth living, he crushes between his fists. He is left with nothing but blood on his hands.

In contrast to other scenes from Hercules' life, the drama and the anguish of this event have largely been avoided by artists. Canova's relief is one of the few moments in Western art when this fatal sequence comes to life. His engagement with the episode is undeniably thoughtful. Canova wants us to see the big picture. In order to do this, he must work in relief. This scene could never have succeeded as an assemblage of sculptures in the round. *Distance* is key. The relief exaggerates a distance that Canova marked out in an earlier painting of the scene. The sign of Hercules' madness lies in his inability to connect with those around him. He is unaware of the children that cling to his legs. He and Megara are unable to touch. Her desperate grasping gesture shows that she knows that intimacy may restore their relationship. Out of sympathy, the flames echo her gesture. Too late, Amphitryon throws out the healing hands that might have brought Hercules back to his senses.

It is the figure of Amphitryon who provides the clue for understanding this scene. Strictly, he should not be there at all. According to tradition, he was killed in the fight against Egrinus. Only one version of the myth involves the frantic intercession of Amphitryon, placing him before an altar of Zeus (in a gesture to his own Pheidian reputation, Canova re-carves Pheidias' lost masterpiece, the statue of Zeus from Olympia, as the cult statue to whom the altar is dedicated). Canova's relief leads us straight back to the most innovative of the Athenian tragedians, Euripides, and his play *Heracles*. Copyists knew this. In engravings of this relief, they even add act and scene numbers. Canova doesn't just want us to look, he wants us to *read*.

Reading Euripides' *Heracles*, we find a much-adapted version of the story. Euripides has altered the sequence of events. According to the standard tradition, Hercules performs his labours as an act of atonement for the murder of his wife and children. Instead, Euripides transports these events to the moment at which Hercules has just finished them. He also introduces a whole series of new events in Thebes. The play begins with the family of Hercules huddling around an altar. There has been regime change in Thebes, and the

46

tyrant Lycus has seized power. Megara and her family are now considered a threat to the new order and are about to be put to death. Hercules is their only hope, but the hero is nowhere to be found. Challenged to retrieve Cerberus, the hound of Hades, Hercules has descended into the Underworld, a journey from which few have ever returned. He seems lost to his family. They have given up hope of him ever returning in time, and prepare for death. However, as they are doing this, Hercules returns triumphant. Not only has he wrestled Cerberus into the daylight, but he has also rescued the hero Theseus from the Underworld. His last, and greatest, labour has been accomplished. However, on his return, he is shocked out of his sense of jubilation by the looks of misery on the faces of his family. Discovering what has happened, he is roused into a fury. He exterminates the tyrant, rescues his own family, and restores order to Thebes. Hercules and his family go inside their house to sacrifice to the gods and celebrate their success.

At this point, when it looks as if disaster has been avoided, Iris, the emissary of Hera, turns up. Accompanying her is the horrid goddess of Madness, Lyssa. A child of Night, Lyssa resembles a Gorgon. Her hair is a mass of hissing vipers. She arrives flying through the air on a stage crane. They have come on the orders of Hera, to afflict Hercules with such a madness that he kills his wife and children. Hera is hoping to bring Hercules to a state of despair, and perhaps even provoke his suicide. Strangely, it is gruesome Lyssa who has most misgivings about the plan. Iris refuses to entertain them. 'Hera did not send you here for your wisdom,' Iris remarks pointedly. And so reluctantly the goddess enters the house and undertakes her horrible duty.

As is traditional in Greek drama, we are spared seeing the bloodshed. Nevertheless, a messenger comes out to give a vivid report. He recounts how Hercules, maddened and convinced that enemies surround him, murders each child in turn, and then turns on his wife. Only Amphitryon escapes. Just as Hercules is about to murder him, Athena decides to put a stop to this horror and, picking up a stone, hurls it at Hercules, knocking him unconscious. As the messenger concludes his speech, the doors of the house open and out on to the stage rolls a platform supporting a scene that could be a pendant to the one that Canova has depicted. Corpses litter the floor. Hercules, bloodstained and unconscious, has been tied to a column by his father.

The rest of the play involves Hercules coming to terms with his terrible acts. He seriously entertains thoughts of suicide. Only the urgent intercessions of his father persuade him to give up the idea. Hercules can see no way forward. It is into this scene of despair that Theseus, the king of Athens, arrives. Rescued by Hercules from the Underworld, he has now come to give the hero succour in his time of need. Eventually, he convinces Hercules that there is more to heroism than fighting monsters. Heroism resides in fulfilling the duties of friendship. These are duties that Hercules can perform by accompanying Theseus to Athens where he will receive purification of the blood-guilt that he has accrued. The play ends with a reluctant, but resigned Hercules accompanying the hero to Athens, and an uncertain future.

The Madness of Hercules

We have already encountered one of Euripides' attempts to turn the Hercules myths into dramatic theatre. His *Alcmene* transformed the story of Hercules' conception into a story of betrayal, suspicion and revenge. In *Heracles*, he turned his attention to the fruit of those unhappy events. In doing so, Euripides was taking a big risk. The stories about Hercules' life were not the usual subject of tragedy. Hercules was undoubtedly popular in the Greek world. Wherever there is a Greek settlement, there is almost always a cult of Hercules. No other hero rivalled him in popularity. Yet, this popularity is not echoed on the tragic stage. He occurs in plenty of comedies. His stupendous appetite sits well with the love of excess that runs through Greek comedy, but he is out of place in tragedy.

Tragedy was a balancing act. It could not strike too close. Events needed to be removed from everyday experience. Tragedies, although they are often involved with aspects of Athenian life, are almost always staged in the remote past in places away from Athens (Argos and Thebes are popular locations). You were playing with fire if you tried to stage a tragedy that depicted contemporary people and events. When the poet Phrynichus staged a tragedy in 492 BC about the recent sacking of the city of Miletus by the Persians, he induced an outbreak of shock and anguish in the theatre. When Athens eventually recovered, it resolved never again to conduct such a dangerous experiment and fined the poet 1,000 drachmas. Tragedy had to confine itself to the realm of the mythic.

At the same time, tragedy needed empathy in order to

be successful. It was not sufficient to recite a series of ancient stories. They needed to be stories with bite. Their characters had to be involved in events that mirrored the concerns, pleasures and anxieties of the ancient city. Tragedy was about the drama of individuals in communities. Hercules, the permanent outsider, had little to offer. Indeed, one of the epithets for Hercules was 'Monoikos', 'the one who dwells alone' (the town of Monaco ultimately derives its name from a shrine to this aspect of the hero). His self-sufficiency cuts him off from making a contribution to drama. It is only when he engages in relationships that the possibility of tragedy is realised. We need the vulnerability that comes through intimacy and engagement. Heroism can be a solitary business. It takes two for tragedy.

In order for tragedy to work, Hercules needs to be not only embedded in a relationship, but also coupled with success. The higher he reaches, the farther he has to fall. The appeal of the Hercules myth is that it offers a character who enjoys success far beyond anything even remotely possible for a mortal, and yet that success still cannot guarantee his happiness. To emphasise the extent of Hercules' fall, Euripides moves the events of his madness from before his labours to after them. No longer is his madness a precursor to his greatest exploits. It now undercuts them. What is the value of fame, if you are unable even to stop yourself killing your wife and children? Virtue has fulfilled her promise. Hercules has secured fame but now it looks like a hollow prize. Maybe he would have been better off plumping for Vice after all.

The Madness of Hercules

This is one of the key issues that runs through the story of Hercules' madness – the value of heroism. Greek tragedy loved staging verbal conflicts between characters. The audience never seems to have tired of dialectic. By having Hercules appear only mid-way through the play, we get an opportunity to hear conflicting views on the hero's life and actions before we see him. As one would expect, the tyrant Lycus is the most critical. He sees no value in killing beasts. True heroism is fighting for your city. There is no honour in the actions that Hercules has performed. His attitude is summed up by his choice of favourite weapon, the bow. Hercules prefers to operate alone, and at a distance. He is not one for joining the ranks of the phalanx. Amphitryon is able to mount a spirited defence of the bow, but Lycus' broader points remain unanswered. Indeed, Hercules himself gives some validity to Lycus' opinions when he arrives home, and realises how his neglect of his family in favour of adventuring has let them get into this predicament. 'So much for my labours. They are nothing compared to the tasks I have to perform here . . . What is worthwhile about killing a hydra or a lion, if I do not prevent the death of my children?' he declares. These words will come back to haunt him.

Euripides has borrowed the general outline of the mythic tradition, and adapted it. Hercules has now defeated not some petty local king, but the forces of death itself. He stands at his greatest capacity. It is a situation that vengeful Hera cannot bear. Hera has remained an incidental figure until now. Her absence from the comic tradition about the conception of Hercules is understandable. Comedy requires everything to be tied up in the end. The happy reconciliation of Jupiter, Alcmena and Amphitryon was the desired result. There is no room for unforgiving spite. There is not much to laugh about in her attempt to stall the pregnancy and her gift of serpents to the newborn babes.

To the Greeks, she was a powerful and fearsome goddess. Her shrines were some of the oldest and most magnificent in the Mediterranean. The temple complex built on the island of Samos was considered one of the marvels of the Greek world. At times she threatens to eclipse even her husband, Zeus. Hera was not the power behind the throne, she was on the throne. In an archaic statue at Olympia, we find Zeus dancing attendance on his wife as she sits firmly ensconced on 'her golden throne'. In another statue, carved by the sculptor Polyclitus, Zeus is reduced to the form of a cuckoo who perches on the shoulder of his enthroned wife. She was capable of great cruelty and monstrous acts. Her humour has a hard edge to it. When a mother once begged the goddess for a blessing for her two outstanding children, Hera immediately put the children into a coma – a 'gift' that spared them the vicissitudes of life. She conceived the smith god Hephaestus as an act of defiance against her husband and then, when she discovered that he was lame, she threw the newborn infant from the heights of Olympus. Two of the most terrible monsters that Hercules ever faced, the hydra and the Nemean lion, were suckled at her breast.

In Greek, Heracles can never escape from Hera. Their names are intertwined. On one interpretation, the name of

Heracles means 'the glory of Hera'. Their reputations are inextricably linked. It is a zero–sum competition. Every time Hercules succeeds, Hera is diminished. He advertises Zeus' infidelity, and thereby shames Zeus' wife. 'I've been pushed out of my place in Heaven by whores,' laments Juno in Seneca's play about the madness of Hercules.

The reputations of gods and men are always competitive. The fame of men inevitably risks occluding the reputation of the gods. Glory-seeking men threaten to steal the prizes from the gods. The pursuit of fame was a dangerous business to the Greek mind. You were more likely to provoke envy than admiration from the divine. The myths of the Greeks were full of stories of mortals who had overstepped the mark, and suffered disastrous consequences as a result. Bellerophon, who tamed Pegasus and defeated the Chimera, became the most 'hated by all the gods' when he attempted to reach Olympus on his winged steed and join their company. Ixion, a king of Thessaly, forgot his place while dining with his patron Zeus. Drunk, he attempted to rape Hera, only to find that he, in fact, had intercourse with an effigy made from clouds. It was not an unproductive coupling. Its offspring are the centaurs (their name means to 'prick wind'). This probably seemed poor consolation to Ixion, though; he was crucified on a fiery wheel for his presumption. Behaviour that would not be out of place for gods will not be tolerated in mortals. The satyr Marsyas, who challenged Apollo to a musical competition, was tied to a tree and flayed alive. So copious was his flow of blood that it gave birth to a river. We have already encountered Niobe, who saw her children murdered by Apollo and Artemis because she dared to take too much pride in their beauty. In a jealous rage, Athena tore the tapestry masterpiece of Arachne to shreds, driving the distraught artist to suicide (and condemning her to an afterlife as a spider).

The gods guard their prerogatives jealously. It is for this reason that Iris, the emissary of Hera, explains that she must drive Hercules mad. 'If he escapes punishment, the gods will be worthless and it is mortals who will be great.' Or as Seneca puts it, 'We must fear for heaven. Having conquered the lowest, he may seize the highest.' The Greeks endowed their gods with an element of their own slave-owner mentality. Like them, the gods enjoyed the services of their servants, but always feared their potential. These underlings threatened to overthrow their masters. Once again, the Hercules myth brings us round to facing some uncomfortable realities about the gods. We have already had a taste of their amorality. Now we get to experience their cruelty.

It was not just the gods who took an interest in the threats posed by those driven by boundless ambition. Such paranoia and envy over a rising star was something to which the Roman philosopher Seneca could relate. He produced his own version of the story, *Hercules Furens*, in the mid first century AD. His interest in the topic of ambition and its consequences was more than academic. His life depended on it. Seneca, tutor and courtier to the Emperor Nero, operated in the midst of a world where political advancement was a game played with deadly consequences. Rivals at court plotted and schemed. Poisonous gossip was poured into the ears of the Emperor. All it took was one misplaced word, one misunderstood look, one joke too many, and imperial wrath would ensure death for the poor, promising unfortunate. Or so the Romans liked to believe.

The terrible anecdotes that they circulated about their rulers titillated them. Imperial depravity, debauchery and brutality, all served to distance the Emperor from the mortal realm, and elevate him to a level with the gods. The Romans might have lost any humanity from the centre of their world, but they were able to replace it with a potency that was directly predicated on the divine. The cornerstone of the Roman world was an individual who increasingly looked and acted like a god.

At least, from a distance. Such anecdotes also circulated because they became the new hard currency among a group who measured power not by the office that you held, but by your proximity to this monstrous core. Knowledge implied access that, in turn, implied power. In the new economy so keenly promoted by these imperial hangers–on, knowing how to run the Emperor became just as much a science as knowing how to run an Empire.

It was not a system that was designed to lessen anxiety. A panacea to soothe this fevered situation or, better yet, calm a troubled imperial brow was desperately needed. Such a thing was what Seneca offered. Given that he lived in a world where one's life could depend on the whim of a tyrant, it is no accident that the topic to which he devoted his longest philosophic treatise was anger. For Seneca, the active life led to unhappiness. Ambition was inevitably coupled with an unhealthy brew of passions and fears. Philosophic contentment was almost irreconcilable with an active political career. A constructive retirement should be seriously considered as an antidote to the feverish environment of the imperial court. It was a philosophy that he acted upon as well as preached. Unable to exert his influence in curbing the passions of the headstrong Nero, Seneca sought retirement from public life in AD 64 at the age of sixty-three.

It is for his ambition, more than anything else, that Hercules should be driven mad. True, Seneca found that there was much to admire in Hercules. His rejection of Vice and her base pleasures, his ability to control his fears, and his dedication to promoting the common good, all made him a figure worthy of admiration. However, Seneca was only too aware that a plan to emulate Hercules was an almost certain recipe for disaster. For all his virtues, Hercules was a dangerous role model because his good deeds were coupled with a desire for greatness and a love of fame. These were the hooks with which Virtue had drawn him to the heroic life. For Seneca, they were barbs that could lead only to unhappiness. To stress this point, Seneca's adaptation of Euripides' play dispenses with the all-too-sensible goddess of Madness. The external causes of Hercules' madness are played down. Juno does promise to send madness upon Hercules, but he seems to be doing a pretty good job of inducing it in himself.

In Seneca's version of the story, Hercules never ceases. He complains about the idleness of his hands. The chorus continually offer advice about the dangers of rushing about. Hercules does not listen. He cannot wait for his next battle. In venturing into the Underworld to release the dead, he indicates that he has no truck with the established order. With fatal pride, he challenges Juno to send her worst monster. He will defeat it. It is a boast which will come back to haunt him.

Oddly, although Seneca offers a diagnosis of Hercules' madness that is consistent with his philosophy, his decision to follow Euripides' play and have Hercules eventually reject suicide as a solution seems distinctly un-Senecan. In antiquity, only Socrates is a more famous suicide than Seneca. Tacitus' description of the Roman philosopher forced to open his veins because of the paranoia of a mad emperor became a standard exemplar in both ancient and modern times for moralising about the wickedness of the Empire. Seneca's own suicide ensures that any discussion of suicide in his works takes on added significance. The decision of his Hercules to endure stands in contrast with the author's own decision over a decade later to end it all. The reason for Hercules' endurance partly lies with Seneca's subject matter. Mythological precedent and Euripides' original text do not allow much room for manoeuvre on this point. Yet, this cannot be a complete explanation. Seneca deliberately chose to adapt Euripides' play. If he wanted to depict Hercules as a suicide, there was much more suitable material around. Sophocles' play *The Women of Trachis*, which features Hercules' death on a funeral pyre, would have been a more suitable choice. A version of this is even attributed to him.

Hercules

What the choice of Hercules to live and the decision of Seneca to die really brings out is how finely balanced is the debate in Seneca's *Hercules Furens*. When Hercules talks of suicide, this is not just an empty expression of grief. It is a real, viable option for the hero. In Seneca's examination of the active life, he has brought us to the point at which the most difficult choices need to be made. There is no easy solution. Choosing to live or die is not as simple as it looks. Seneca wants to make us aware that every breath we continue to take has consequences. 'It takes a whole life to learn how to die,' Seneca remarks in his essay *On the Brevity of Life*.

Now that Seneca has put ethics firmly on to the agenda, we might think about the ethical dilemmas involved in viewing Canova's frieze. Where does his art take us? What do we learn? One question that we might ask ourselves is why is it that Canova has depicted the one scene that the audiences of Seneca and Euripides would have been spared. Classical drama took a passionate interest in the consequences of violence. Every possible version of familial murder was rehearsed on the classical stage. Oedipus murders his father. Clytemnestra kills her spouse. Medea slaughters her children. Hercules, as always excessive, attempts the murder of all three. However, in every case, Greek drama refuses to show the act. Such squeamishness seems unusual in a culture that happily performs regular blood sacrifice of animals, the torture of slaves and the occasional murder of prisoners of war. A variety of explanations has been offered for this strange aversion to dramatic violence. The religious origins of tragedy, fears about pollution, problems with staging, and the effect of seeing violence in such intense performances are all possible answers. A combination of these is probably right. Strangely, though, the reverse of the question is not often asked. Rather than asking why the Greeks did not act out violence on stage, we might like to ask why we get such a thrill from doing so.

It is undeniable that there is a terrible beauty in Canova's depiction of Hercules' acts of madness. He is heroically nude while all around him are clothed, and it is hard not to admire his splendid physique. Looking at his sculptured torso, we see simultaneously perfected beauty and a perfected killing machine. It is the same with Canova's depiction of Hercules and Lichas. The horror of the scene cannot mask its marvellous symmetry and movement. They wrest from us a sick admiration. Viewers are trapped in a complicit voyeurism. Should this worry us?

As a piece of dramatic performance, Hercules' madness is as wonderful as it is terrifying. It certainly wowed Renaissance and Enlightenment audiences, who saw no problem in enjoying such scenes. The prevalence of productions and translations of Seneca effected the transmission of the story of Hercules' madness. For a number of years, scenes of madness were in vogue. There was something to be gained by adding 'Furens' to your title, and an episode of raving into your script. The story was even turned into an opera by Melani to celebrate the wedding of Cosimo Medici III in 1661. At first sight, scenes of domestic violence make a strange choice for a wedding celebration, even if they are set to ballet music. Yet their use here provides a clear indication of the way in which these scenes were enjoyed for their dramatic potential far more than their content.

To the Renaissance mind, the cause of such madness could be ascribed equally to an imbalance in humours as to divine intervention or the consequences of overarching ambition. Indeed, there has long been a tendency to read Seneca's virtuoso description of the onset of Hercules' madness (the sudden descent into darkness, the delusions and flashing lights) and diagnose him with a fashionable illness. Hercules has been identified as suffering everything from melancholia to epilepsy and bipolar depression. Seventeenth-century physicians even recommended a 'sleep cure' for madness based on the period of unconsciousness experienced by Hercules before he regained his sanity. Such a period of oblivion they reasoned allowed the black bile that had ascended from the stomach to the brain to be breathed out. Just as the inmates of insane asylums would later be used to provide entertainment to passing do-gooders, so scenes of madness on stage functioned as enjoyable spectacle.

Yet as the anecdote about Caesar which began this chapter reminds us, there are consequences of revelling in this madness. In losing our humanity, we also critique our heroism. As noted before, Euripides made the murder of his wife and children the climax of Hercules' labours while a competing tradition preferred to make it the start. In fact, it does not really matter where you place these crimes. The important thing is the realisation that the death of his wife and children are inevitably linked to his murders of Greece's greatest monsters. Watching the labours should not make us too comfortable. Those arrows that can kill a centaur really rip through female flesh. The vice-like grip that can choke off the windpipe of a lion works even better on the supple gullet of a child.

CHAPTER FOUR

Greek Adventures

Hercules' murder of his wife and children requires exculpation. For the Greeks, murder was not just a crime, it was a form of impiety. It was an interruption in the natural order that needed a religious remedy. The blood of the victim clung to the hands of the killer. Even accidental death required cleansing. In Athens, if a block of stone fell from a building and killed someone, it was put on trial. If found 'guilty', the stone suffered a form of ritual exile: it was taken and thrown outside the borders of the state. Failure to purify oneself properly after a killing put not only the killer at risk, but also the whole community. Religious pollution was thought to spread like a contagion. It could be transmitted through physical contact or even proximity. Athenian jurors were afraid to occupy the same enclosed space as a killer and arranged for all their murder trials to be held in the open air. Plague, sterility, famine and attack by avenging spirits were just some of the penalties that the unclean suffered. For those whose crimes could not be purified within the city, exile was the only option.

The need for atonement produces great art. Greek tragedy thrives on stories of exiles wandering in search of release and purification from their crimes. Orestes plagued by the Furies for the murder of his mother, Clytemnestra, seeks purification from Apollo. Even driving pins into his eyes cannot assuage Oedipus' guilt. His eyes have seen too much. The burden of incest and murder pushes him ever onwards. Blind, he hobbles through Greece looking for rest.

It is this group of outcasts that Hercules joins. Too unclean even to bury his children, he leaves Thebes to seek someone who can wash away his pollution. Tradition varies as to who performed the ritual of purification. In Euripides' *Heracles*, the act was performed by Theseus, the king of Athens, a sign of the friendship that Theseus argues makes life endurable in face of the cruelty of the gods. This is almost certainly the invention of the tragedian. Athens was rapacious in acquiring events for its own mythic history; there were few stories that it could not plunder and rework for its own ends. A wider consensus favours Thespius, while other candidates include Sicalus and Nausithous the Phaeacian. Whoever performed the deed matters little, what is important is the outcome. Hercules was purified, but at a price.

The logic of the purification ritual was that blood was

washed away with blood. The precise form that the purification ritual took varied from place to place, but central to all these rituals was the sacrifice of an animal (usually a pig), and the subsequent sprinkling of its blood on the hands of the killer. Yet for Hercules the blood that washed away the stain of murder was just the start of more bloodshed.

After his purification Hercules consulted the Pythia, the oracular priestess of Apollo at Delphi, about where it was appropriate for him to live in exile. It was only natural that he should consult her for such advice. One of the modern misconceptions about Greek oracles is that they were designed to tell the future, but such consultations, if they occurred, were the exception. The function of oracles was to act as intermediaries between man and the gods. Their main business was to advise about the correct performance of religious rituals and to determine which acts would be pleasing and which would be insulting to the divinities. You consulted oracles not to find out who was going to win the chariot race at the next Olympic Games, but to determine what sacrifices to make if your horse won.

Even in his purified state, Hercules was still a potential source of pollution that needed to be handled carefully. The oracle's decision to send him into the service of King Eurystheus of Tiryns not only made logical sense to the ancient Greek mind, it also provided a convenient pretext for some of the most famous chapters in the Hercules saga. Oddly, the purification of Hercules marks the beginning of his life as a killer. This time, not of men, but monsters. Eurystheus, driven by envy and egged on by Hera, sends

Hercules out to perform increasingly impossible tasks against monstrous foes.

Eurystheus had already played a part in the life of Hercules. Zeus had wished the kingdom of Tiryns to pass to Hercules and had promised it to the first born of his children. However, while Alcmena lay thrashing about in the pains of labour, Hera had ensured that Eurystheus, another descendant of Zeus, had his birth eased forward, and so obtained the kingdom. Once again, the king of the gods was tricked by his wily wife. Indeed, much of Greek myth reads like a domestic comedy. Through the intrigues of the gods, we learn important lessons about male omnipotence/impotence, especially in the household.

The Greeks enjoyed the spectacle of the powerful experiencing reverses: Zeus, the ruler of the gods, who proved unable to rule his own household; Oedipus, whose quick brain helped him win the kingdom of Thebes, but could not solve a murder mystery in which he was the killer; Apollo, who was sold into servitude for killing the Cyclops. And Hercules, the most powerful man in the Greek world, who was forced to fetch and carry for a ruler who had cheated him out of his birthright. In some versions of the story, it was this obligation that sent him mad in the first place.

In the ancient world the most famous depiction of the labours that Hercules performed for King Eurystheus was on the temple of Zeus at Olympia. This temple, whose gold and ivory statue of Zeus was one of the Seven Wonders of the World, occupied a central place in the life of mainland

Greece. Pilgrims and state delegations came from all over to visit. Its festival of games was famous. The only universally accepted system of measuring time in the Greek world was based on counting the number of times that the Olympic Games had been held since their inception in (supposedly) 776 BC. A universal truce was observed so that participants could travel to and from the Games.

The temple of Zeus was begun around 470 BC and completed before 456 BC. During this period Olympia was under the control of the nearby town of Elis. The construction of the temple was funded through a combination of war-booty derived by expansionist Elis' conquest of its neighbours and income from the Olympic Games. Just as today, the Olympic Games were an economic phenomenon as well as an athletic one. Revenues from fees, donations and the assorted expenditure of festival visitors poured into the Elean coffers. This temple was such an architectural triumph that jealous Athens felt it must rival it. Not to be outdone, the Athenians made their rival temple – the Parthenon – longer, wider and fractionally taller. The architect of the temple of Zeus was a local, Libon of Elis. The style was Doric. One of the distinctive features of this style, in addition to its thick, squat columns, is the presence of an entablature with a frieze of marble panels, often decorated, called metopes.

It is through a series of these decorated slabs that the story of the labours is told. The slabs that depict the life of Hercules were divided into two groups of six, one placed above the portico that provided the main entrance to the temple, the other in a similar position at the back of the temple. Remains of these sculptures were first discovered by a French archaeological team in 1829 and fragments are shared between Greek museums and the Louvre.

'The Twelve Labours of Hercules' has become such an accepted part of our vocabulary and thinking that it is easy to miss the arbitrariness of this temple decoration. In looking at these metopes we are not examining a representation of the 'Twelve Labours'. Instead, we are probably seeing the moment in which they came into existence. The construction of the list of the twelve labours of Hercules is certainly

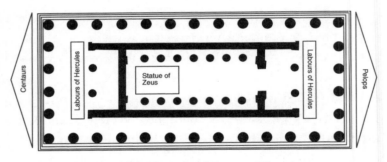

Plan of the Temple of Zeus at Olympia.

a late addition to an already mature body of stories about the hero. Indeed, it may well be the case that the number of labours was originally ten, and then later increased to twelve. These differing traditions on the number of labours can be reconciled by a story that King Eurystheus discounted two labours, the defeat of the hydra and the cleansing of the Augean stables, on the grounds that Hercules received either

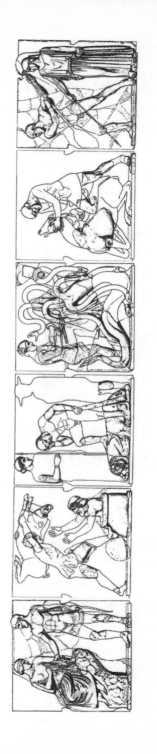
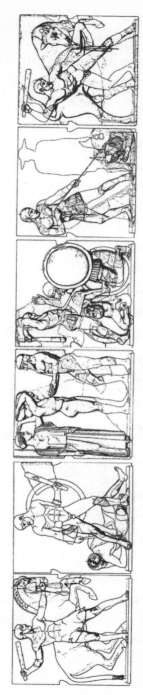

Reconstruction of the metopes from the Temple of Zeus at Olympia.

payment or help for them, and that therefore, although he carried out twelve tasks, there were only ten official labours.

It seems likely that it was the fame of this sculptural arrangement, combined with a series of historical accidents, that led to these metopes creating the canonical list. If another series of depictions had captured the imagination of ancient mythographers, we would have had a different number and list of labours. If, for example, they had followed the decorative scheme of the Treasury of the Athenians at Delphi then we would have had only five labours. Hercules' battle with Cycnus, one of the sons of Ares, would have been elevated to one of the important mythological stories rather than being relegated as it is now to a minor adventure, remembered only at Delphi and in an epic verse fragment and a number of vase-paintings. Similarly, Hercules' quest for the cattle of Geryon, which dominates the Delphi metopes, would also have been regarded as of much greater importance.

There is even some suggestion that the citizens of Elis were able to use the prominence of the temple of Zeus at Olympia to sneak one of their own local stories about Hercules into the list. The cleansing of the Augean stables is a local story from Elis that seems to be given little prominence until it appears on the temple of Zeus. By elevating it on to the frieze of the temple, the Eleans were able to bring it to the attention of the wider Greek public and fix it into Greek imagination.

Visitors to the metopes today get a vastly different experience from the pilgrims of ancient Greece. Viewing architectural sculpture in a museum poses problems. Firstly, one is always standing too close. These sculptures were intended to be seen from a distance and at an angle. So, for example, the most famous architectural sculptures, the Parthenon marbles, were up high, poorly lit, and probably went unnoticed by a large number of visitors to the Parthenon. Certainly, none of the ancient accounts mentions the frieze. Secondly, seeing these sculptures stripped from the building and their accompanying decoration, we lose any sense of the way in which the sculptures interacted with the building and each other. It is easy to forget that each element acted in concert with others to create messages for the viewer.

Nor were the metopes the only, or indeed the primary, sculptural decoration on the temple. They competed and collaborated with the pedimental sculptures that graced each end of the temple and the colossal statue of Zeus that dwelt inside it. Hercules provides both a physical and conceptual link between these various works.

To the visitor to the temple the two most obvious sculptural groups were those located in the pediments at either end of the temple. Apart from their interest in rivalry, conflict and competition (appropriate enough themes at the site of the Olympic Games), the two pediments have little in common. In the east pediment we find a local story, the chariot race between Pelops and Oinomaus. The west pediment depicts a tale from the far north of Greece, the battle between Lapiths and centaurs.

The story of the chariot race is not a happy tale. The

prize was Hippodameia, the only daughter of King Oinomaus of Pisa. Oinomaus had received a prophecy that he would die at the hands of his son-in-law. To prevent such an event occurring, he organised a chariot race between himself and any suitors. The suitor loaded Hippodameia on to his chariot and set off. If Oinomaus caught up with the pair, the unfortunate suitor was speared to death. Thirteen suitors had already tried to outrun the king and failed by the time a mysterious foreigner, Pelops, arrived to chance his hand.

It is the moment before the start of this fateful race that is captured in the pediment. The two chariot teams are marshalled and Zeus himself is present to witness the events. He stands between the two competitors, dividing the composition. In this tableau's perfect symmetry, we sense the calm before the storm. The impending disaster is confirmed by the seer who sits behind the chariot of Oinomaus. The future he sees clearly distresses him. He raises his hand in dismay and despair.

What he senses is that this race will prove fatal to Oinomaus. Pelops, unable to win by skill, has bribed Oinomaus' charioteer to substitute wax lynch-pins for the metal ones on the king's chariot. During the race, the wheels will come off and Oinomaus will be killed. However, this is just the start of the tragic sequence of events. Pelops will refuse to honour his bargain with the charioteer and will murder the duplicitous servant. As he drowns him, the servant will call down a curse on Pelops and all of his line.

The price for Pelops' actions falls on to his descendants.

Each generation feels it differently. The blood feud between his children, Atreus and Thyestes, will result in child-murder, cannibalism and incest, while his grandchild, Agamemnon, will send the whole Greek world to war at Troy, murder his daughter and, in turn, be murdered by his wife. This final act initiates a new cycle of bloodshed as Agamemnon's children, Orestes and Electra, avenge his death, but in the process commit one of the most heinous crimes – matricide. The misfortunes of the house of Pelops were revisited by the Greeks in countless works of literature and art. In a very real sense almost all Greek tragedy rests on the lynch-pins of Oinomaus' chariot.

The story of the west pediment involves us in another tragic genealogy. We have already met Ixion, whose attempt to rape Hera resulted in the production of the race of cen-taurs and his subsequent crucifixion. Here we find a confrontation between his two sets of offspring. The location of the battle is the wedding feast of Ixion's son Peirithoos, King of the Lapiths, and Hippodameia, daughter of Atrax. As relatives and neighbours, the centaurs had grudgingly been invited. Things had gone well until the centaurs, mad-dened by drink, attempted to abduct the women and boys. The lust of the centaurs was legendary. In a nod to their over-sexed nature, some depictions even feature them with two sets of genitals – one between their front legs as in a man, another between their hind legs as in a horse. The ensuing battle in which the Lapiths fought off the centaurs was a popular motif in Greek temple decoration. Like other examples, this pediment relishes the violence of the

encounter. Hair is pulled. Ears ripped. Female breasts bru-
tally grabbed. One centaur bites deep into the arm of a
struggling Lapith.

Against these two very different images – one full of
frantic action, the other icily calm – we need to place the
labours of Hercules. In the way in which they intersect with
both pediments, they provide some unity to the sculptural
programme. The adventures of Hercules are an appropriate
choice for decorating this temple not only because he was the
mythical founder of the Olympic Games, but also because he
has something to say to both these scenes. His labours provide
counterpoints to both images. Hercules' battles underline
and contrast with the meaninglessness of the violence of the
centaurs. His fights are no drunken brawls. At the same time,
he problematises the violence. In the course of his career,
Hercules will battle both Lapiths and centaurs. He shows
that neither side in this fight is unquestionably good or evil.
He introduces a note of ambiguity into the scene. Blame lies
on both sides for this wedding disaster. In their reluctant
invitation the Lapiths failed as hosts; the centaurs failed as
guests. Hercules reminds us that the rules of hospitality
require genuine commitment on both sides.

Hercules provides an alternative to the tragedy which
the chariot race of Pelops sets up. Hercules is also a descendant of Pelops as both his mother and his adopted father can
claim descent from Pelops' line. The Herculean sculptures
give us the flip side of suffering – that such tragedy produces
not only art, but also fame and, even occasionally, triumph.
We potentially lose much if we follow the seer's example

and just throw up our hands in despair. Indeed, Hercules' labours provide an interlude, a break in the curse of the house of Pelops. The ghastly hostility between Atreus and Thyestes will erupt only as they fight to succeed Eurystheus as King of Tiryns. While Eurystheus still possesses the throne, and keeps setting tasks for Hercules, that dread day is avoided.

These sculptures then encourage us to think and tell stories. This is particularly the case with the Hercules metopes. Their mannered designs with their strong diagonal and vertical lines draw our attention to issues of deliberation and reflection. There is no artlessness in their art. We sense minds at work, wanting to make contact. These sculptures demand interpretation. None of the metopes stands on its own as a complete and intelligible account of the labours. Each sculpture requires explanation. Unless we know the story of the Stymphalian birds or the cleansing of the Augean stables we will be unable to work out why Hercules seems to be handing a brace of ducks to Athena or digging up some earth at her command. The metopes function as a sculptural shorthand for the labours. They are an *aide-mémoire* to stories that you already should have absorbed. They want to set up an epic in your head.

So let us play along with the conceit of these sculptures and listen to the stories that they want us to hear. Unfortunately, the precise order in which the metopes were displayed is conjectural. Our best source for the sculptures of the temple of Zeus at Olympia is the pilgrim-cum-travel-writer Pausanias. Unfortunately, by the time he wrote his account in the second century AD, severe earthquake damage had resulted in numerous repairs and the restoration of the metopes out of their original order. However, if we postulate that each metope was designed to be seen from a certain point of view, and that this is reflected in their composition, then a tentative reconstruction of the original order is possible.

If we begin at the west end of the temple, we can be reasonably certain that two of the most famous labours of Hercules occupied the central positions. On the right was the scene depicting Hercules' triumph over the Nemean lion and next to it his battle against the hydra. Hercules' defeat of the lion of Nemea is conventionally his first labour. We find the creature lying dead at Hercules' feet. Hercules rests exhausted, leaning on his club. Yet, the presence of the club is a little misleading. This feat is one achieved not with weapons, but with Hercules' bare hands. One of the distinguishing features of the labours is that they are not just marvels of brawn, they also require brain. The feature that made the Nemean lion so dangerous was not its ferocity, but its invulnerability to weapons. No blade could puncture its skin. Hercules overcame this by jettisoning his weapons and wrestling and choking the monster to death.

This tussle of man against beast with its concomitant associations of nature versus culture has appealed to artists from antiquity onwards. It particularly resonated with a world in which wrestling was a prized sport. Bold Greek athletes would even take on lions in imitation of their wrestling hero. In numerous Greek vases, we see Hercules in wrestling pose, each straining muscle picked out with obvious delight, going head to head with the lion. Yet, the obvious voyeuristic pleasures to be had from this scene have been eschewed by the sculptor. He has chosen one seemingly from when all the action is over.

There are, perhaps, two reasons for this. The first is that it allows him to add and stress the presence at the scene of the two assisting deities, Athena and Hermes. (It is worth remembering at the outset of the labours that without divine assistance and favour nothing is possible. This is a journey that Hercules cannot make on his own.) The second aspect that the sculpture stresses is Hercules' ingenuity rather than his strength. The informed viewer knows that this labour is not over yet. Hercules has been dispatched not just to kill the lion, but also to bring back its skin. In many ways this is an even more impossible task than killing the beast. How do you skin an animal if no blade can puncture its flesh? It is this dilemma that our hero faces in this scene. Hercules' solution is a masterstroke – he skins the creature using its own claws to cut the flesh.

Such ingenuity is also displayed in the second labour, Hercules' battle against the hydra. If the previous image presented us with the quiet repose after the struggle, this panel reminds us of the frantic energy each labour requires. It has not escaped the artist that the most important feature of this labour is the hydra's heads. The panel is a riot of snapping, hissing jaws. The precise number of heads that this monstrous water-snake possessed was debated. Some sources give nine heads, others one hundred. Only a sceptic like

Hercules

Pausanias thought it had one head. All the rest of our sources agree that it had multiple heads and that removing one caused several others to grow in its place. It was only when Hercules started to cauterise the necks after decapitation that he could put a stop to this hideous regeneration. In the relief sculpture, we find him mid-decapitation. He holds a knife in one hand and a blazing torch in the other. However, not even butchering the serpent in this way could quite put an end to it. According to one tradition, one head was immortal and could be eliminated only by Hercules burying it under a rock.

The interesting thing about this panel is what is missing. As reconstructions of this relief show, the performance of simultaneous decapitation and cauterisation is an awkward affair. Even within the serenity of classical aesthetics, we can sense the tension. The hydra is a live, writhing mass. In contrast, even with only the pitiful few fragments of Hercules that remain, his form seems frozen and wooden. It is no wonder that he soon acquires a companion to assist him in his labours. It is with this labour that we see the start of one of the important relationships in Hercules' life, that with Iolaus, the son of Hercules' half-brother Iphicles. According to an arrangement that will become the dominant tradition, it is Iolaus who will cauterise the stumps once Hercules lops the heads off. However, it is not only Hercules' companion who is left out of this scene. The hydra also enjoyed assistance. While Hercules struggled with the beast, he was constantly harried by a crab who pinched his feet. Indeed, for this service, Hera would eventually

78

raise the crab to a constellation in the sky – the constellation of Cancer.

The final element in the story that is missing is the important aftermath. Having slain the hydra, Hercules then dips his arrows in its blood, coating them with one of the most fearsome poisons in Greek myth. Even the slightest contact was fatal, the victim perishing in agony.

Hercules' arrows come to exercise a fascination in the ancient mind, and developing arrows with a potency to rival his was a common fantasy. Arrowheads in the ancient world were regularly treated with snake venom and other poisons intended to promote infection and disease. Writers were constantly on the look-out for stories about fabulous recipes by which they could make their arrows even more deadly. Indeed, the strange arms race that the stories of Hercules' arrows inspired has caused one critic to dub him the 'father of bio-chemical warfare'.

While the first two labours demonstrate features that we readily associate with Hercules – strength and bravery – the next labour is evidence of an entirely different set of resources: speed and diplomacy. The relief shows Hercules wrestling with a hind. This splendid beast endowed with gold horns was the property of the goddess Artemis (Lat. Diana), virgin huntress and twin sister of Apollo. Indeed, there may have been an inscription on the horns proclaiming this. Even without the gold or the inscription, the horns are odd. Few female deer possess horns apart from reindeer. And while there has been some suggestion that reindeer lie behind the myth of Hercules and the hind, the sex of the deer more likely owes its origin to its guardian, Artemis.

Its associations with Artemis are strengthened by its normal habit, the wilds of Arcadia. The animal is conventionally referred to as the Cerynitian hind after the river Cerynites which flows through Arcadia and Achaia. This wild region was conventionally one of Artemis' stamping grounds and a number of the stories associated with her are located here. All of these make her a goddess whom one should be fearful of crossing. The most famous of these concerns the hunter Acteon who, having been discovered watching the goddess while she bathes, is turned into a stag and torn apart by his own hunting dogs. It is worth remembering this story next time you see one of the statues of bathing goddesses in a museum. To the ancient viewer part of the thrill that they obtained from looking at these statues was not only the pleasure of seeing the naked form, but knowing that unlike Acteon they could watch a naked goddess and get away with it.

It is the potential threat from Artemis that hangs over this labour. Ordered by Eurystheus to obtain the animal for him, Hercules pursues it for a year before he manages to wrestle it to the ground. Unlike the previous two metopes which show Hercules' opponents either wounded or dead, here the beast is very much alive. It is his preservation of the beast which allows Hercules to escape this labour unscathed. By refusing to kill the animal and releasing it once he had shown it to Eurystheus, Hercules manages to avoid offending Artemis. According to one version, he even manages to convince the goddess that the blame for his actions does not lie with him, but with Eurystheus, who ordered him to capture the hind.

Certainly, the sculptor of the metopes seems to think that there was something ridiculous about Eurystheus' requests. The accompanying metope shows Hercules returning with the next beast that he had been asked to retrieve, the Erymanthian boar. Eurystheus is so alarmed by the prospect of confronting the beast that he attempts to hide in a storage jar in the ground. Not to be deterred, Hercules appears ready to drop the boar on top of him.

This scene plays with the comic reversal of the weak, foolish king and the strong, capable servant. Eurystheus is shown up for giving orders, but not being able to handle their consequences. The image of Eurystheus hiding in his storage jar was a popular one in antiquity. We find it on vases and sculptures throughout the Greek world. On a treasury at Silaris near Paestum, we find it replicated in sandstone.

However, as is often the case, comedy hides tragedy. Boar hunting was not a business entered upon lightly. Usually, when characters in Greek literature embark on such a hunt, somebody ends up dead. So it is with this labour. The story of the Erymanthian boar is a tale with a tragic twist, for it was in the pursuit of this beast that Hercules' envenomed arrows would claim the lives of two of the noblest centaurs. As we have already seen from the west pediment, centaurs could be wild, bestial creatures. There were two exceptions, Chiron and Pholos. The more famous of the two was Chiron. Wise and skilled in medicine, he was the tutor to both Achilles and Asclepius.

It is uncontrolled appetite – on the part of both Hercules and the other centaurs – which leads to the pair's deaths. Hercules stopped with Pholos on his journey to the mountain of Erymanthus. Unable to restrain his thirst, he asks Pholos to break open the vat of wine shared by the centaurs. Pholos tries to warn him that the smell of wine will attract other centaurs, but Hercules presses him to open it anyway. Unable to resist this aroma, the centaurs arrive, armed and ready for a brawl. In the ensuing conflict, which spills over into the home of Pholos' neighbour, Chiron, Hercules fires his arrows at one of the violent creatures, only to see it pass through its arm and stick fast in Chiron's knee. Normally, death would be instantaneous. However, Chiron possesses the gift of immortality, which in this case proves to be a mixed blessing. Unable to die, he is forced to endure agony as the poison of the hydra courses through his body. Washing out the poison does no good. According to one tradition, it was this attempt that gave the waters of the Anigrus river their horrible smell. Release comes only when another agrees to take on the burden of Chiron's immortality. That figure is the other paragon of perpetual suffering, Prometheus, who was chained to a rock for stealing fire from the gods and giving it to man. There his liver is daily pecked out by an eagle only to re-grow each night. It is partly out of a sense of his debt to Chiron that Hercules eventually kills the eagle and frees Prometheus.

However, Hercules' arrows have not finished working their evil. Pholos, amazed by the potency of the arrows, picks one out of a corpse, but accidentally drops it on his foot. He dies instantly. The body of either Pholos or Chiron forms the basis for the Centaur constellation in the sky.

While the return of the Erymanthian boar shows up Eurystheus' poverty as a leader, the next labour, the cleansing of the Augean stables, demonstrates the way in which Hercules and Eurystheus are trapped in a relationship of mutual humiliation. One of the things that the stories of Eurystheus and Hercules explore is the relationship between master and slave, ruler and ruled, and in a hierarchical slave-owning society it was certainly a relationship worth exploring. By getting things so wrong, they hope to show how it might be possible to get things right.

It is clear that shifting mountains of dung from the largest stables in Greece is a task that is beneath Hercules, and the imposition of the time limit of a day does nothing to make it any less so. Hercules' triumph in this labour lies in his ability to avoid contact with the muck himself. His diversion of the rivers Alpheus and Peneus through the stalls washes them clean without the hero having to get his hands too dirty.

The rejection of the mucky aspect of this labour can be seen in the metope. Here the artist shifts attention away from the stables to the act of river diversion. With a strong diagonal composition, he represents the goddess Athena showing the hero where to dig. The introduction of Athena in this metope carries on the theme of divine favour begun in the depiction of Hercules' conquest of the Nemean lion.

It is a theme that is continued throughout the rest of the

metopes. Athena's presence at the labour of the stables is balanced by the metope at the north end of the sequence, the depiction of Hercules with the Stymphalian birds. Here the relationship with the goddess is foregrounded. This time Hercules is offering up his prize not to Eurystheus, but to Athena herself. In many ways the dedication is appropriate. It was Athena's gift of a bronze rattle that allowed Hercules to scare the birds from their dwelling place on the Stymphalian lake and into the sky where he could shoot them down. Her calm, assured acceptance of the birds contrasts with Eurystheus' panic at the sight of the Erymanthian boar. She knows how to handle monsters. Although smaller in size than the boar, these fowl were equally deadly. According to a tradition preserved in a number of places, these birds possessed the ability to fire out their feathers like arrows. Even Pausanias, who doubts many of the labours performed by Hercules, says that the birds of this region are so fierce that armour is no protection against them and that they are fearless attacking even lions and leopards.

Hercules' triumph over the Stymphalian birds ends the metopes on the western end of the temple. To find out the rest of the story we need to move to the eastern end. This is one of the functions of the metopes, they make us move around the building. However, in dividing into sections, they also invite us to pause and reflect on the meaning of the stories that we have told ourselves. Certainly, the value of the labours is something that is worth reflecting upon. This point is underlined by the tendency of these metopes (unlike other sculptural representations of the labours) to celebrate the contemplative moment when the labour is finished. Throughout this narrative one of the things that the metopes of the temple at Olympia ask us to do is think about the value of attributes beyond mere physical prowess. Ingenuity, diplomacy, the relationship between mortals and divine are aspects that have been investigated in the labours. There is a sense that the labours are more than just a series of battles against monsters.

If we need reminding about how far the metopes at Olympia take us from seeing Hercules' achievements in purely physical terms, then we need look no further than the representation of these same labours offered up by France's most famous statesman, Cardinal Richelieu. In a spectacular canvas commissioned by the Cardinal, brutality and blood-shed, the mire of heroism, occupy centre-stage. Here, if the actual labours of Hercules stretch anything, it must be our appetite for gore. Long assumed to be by Correggio, the piece is now identified as the work of Claude Vignon. It most probably occupied a central position in an antechamber at Château Richelieu.

Hercules had long been a favourite of French royal commissions. Henri IV had adopted the hero's image for use in his propaganda. Dubreuil had painted twenty-seven scenes from the life of Hercules in Fontainebleau in 1595. Nicolas Poussin was commissioned to produce a series of decorations for the Grande Galérie of the Louvre based on the life and exploits of Hercules. His final designs divided the life into thirty-six episodes, and, had they been completed, would have stretched from the Palais du Louvre to the Tuileries.

Hercules

Yet, even by the standards of the fondness for Hercules that existed within the French court, Richelieu's self-identification with the hero is striking. It is also understandable.

Even before Dumas transformed him into the moustache-twirling villain of *The Three Musketeers*, Richelieu was as much a character of myth as Hercules. His rise seemed inexorable and his powers were rumoured to border on the supernatural. Initially as secretary of state for foreign affairs and later as prime minister, he transformed France into one of the major European powers. He reformed the administration, crushed numerous rebellions, sorted out palace coups, and expanded French interests in Africa and the Caribbean. He ended the Protestant threat to the kingdom. He also oversaw a revitalisation of French culture, particularly the theatre. He founded the Académie Française, and occupies an important place in the history of the Sorbonne.

It is understandable that in grasping for a metaphor by which this enigmatic figure might be made comprehensible, people settled upon Hercules. It was a conceit that Richelieu was very happy to encourage. Théophraste Renaudot, the father of French journalism, in a poetic homage (1627) refers to him as the 'Hercules Gaulois'. Jean de Routrou, one of the five leading dramatists patronised by Richelieu, wrote his *L'Hercule mourant* (1636) in honour of the Cardinal. Within the Cardinal's residences at Poitou and Reuil, Hercules regularly appears in sculptural decoration. Vignon's painting was not the only scene of Hercules' life in the Palais Richelieu. Charles Le Brun was commissioned to execute a large canvas showing *Hercules Vanquishing the Mares of*

Diomedes (1640–41) and a scene of Hercules on his pyre.

Yet, it is in Vignon's painting that the identification of Richelieu with Hercules is clearest. The work is a series of puns and allusions to the Cardinal. The game starts even before you reach the painting. Surrounding it was a series of decorative anagrams based on Richelieu's name. One pair showed that out of 'Armandus Richeleus' came 'Hercules Admirandus', while in the other 'Armand de Richelieu' was nothing other than the 'ardue main d'Hercule'.

This joking interplay between Hercules and Richelieu continues within the painting. The over-elaborate painted border acts as a signpost to the fact that the real subject of this painting is the Cardinal. The scarlet cords that run through the border and support the cornucopia are references to his office, the anchors at the bottom allude to his role as Superintendent of Shipping and Commerce, while the three ducal coronets relate to his titles. Finally, all of this wraps a lush, rich landscape. We are being treated literally to a 'riche lieu'.

This painting is striking as much for what it tells us about the labours of Hercules as for what it says about the megalomaniac tendencies of France's first minister. Hercules stands in the middle of the picture, Christ-like. He glows with vitality. He looks towards the sky in an act of devotion. In the corner of the scene, we see Juno escaping as fast as she can in a flying chariot. Hercules' smile is benign.

As our eyes drift downwards, we begin to see a scene that might cause us to feel less easy about the beatific smile. The 'riche lieu' turns out to be a charnel house. Corpses litter the scene as far as the eye can see. Hercules' claim to divinity turns out to be solely based on slaughter. The painting replays the labours we have seen, but as a splatter-fest. The whole fabulous bestiary of classical mythology is there, murdered for our enjoyment.

This painting confronts us with the problem that the more intellectual and philosophical fans of Hercules have always tried to avoid – the reduction of Hercules' heroism to a bloodbath. This canvas reveals what the metopes of the temple of Zeus are keen to hide. Namely, that it is all too easy to see the labours of Hercules as not ethical or emotional battles, but physical ones. The labours do not necessarily make Hercules a better person, just a more famous one. He gains his fame because he can kill. Every depiction of the labours of Hercules needs to try hard to avoid repeating this fact.

CHAPTER FIVE

Labours in Far-off Lands

In the end, it was the rains that defeated Alexander the Great in his conquest of India. After trudging through the monsoons of the Punjab, the thought of crossing the swollen river Hyphasis proved too much. His men rebelled and refused to go another step further. His words on this occasion are supplied by the second-century AD Greek historian and Roman senator Arrian:

> You all know that had our forefather Hercules remained in Tiryns or Argos or gone no further than the Peloponnese, or Thebes, he would never have obtained enough glory to achieve the transition from man to God . . . Yet we have passed Nyssa. The Aornus rock which Hercules could not take, we now

possess. Come now add to your possessions the rest
of Asia.

Such bold words fell on deaf ears. Alexander's men were not
prepared to be casualties on his march to godhead. Yet, if the
spirit of Hercules was not enough to move his men, it was
certainly enough for their young Macedonian leader. These
words chime with the grandiose ambition and self-perception
of the man. Alexander was always striving to step out of history into myth. It was a pose that his close companions
whose fortunes depended on his successes were prepared to
indulge and, after his untimely death, perpetuate. From the
moment he stepped on to the shores of Turkey and organised funeral games at the tomb of Achilles, Alexander
signalled that his campaign was going to be an epic battle,
one to rival the Trojan War. Indeed, as Alexander progressed
through Asia even comparisons with the Trojan War started
to look inadequate. His claim of descent from Hercules was
one way of articulating both the magnitude and the novelty
of his enterprise. There was only one hero who could rival
Alexander in the geographic spread of his achievements.

One of the distinguishing features of the later labours is
their location outside mainland Greece, on the fringes of the
'known world'. As we resume our journey round the temple
of Zeus at Olympia, there is a noticeable change in the
nature of the labours. Each story becomes more elaborate.
Each labour consists of a series of minor adventures and tri-
umphs; the line between where the labour begins and ends
starts to blur.

Our circumnavigation of the temple has brought us to its entrance. The labours we will now consider frame our encounter with divinity. Temples were considered the homes of the gods, not places of worship. Indeed, most worship occurred outside a temple at the various altars which surrounded them, and on which sacrifices were made. The cult statues located inside the temples were objects of veneration, but one's encounters with them were largely mediated by rituals. They were objects to be wary of, they possessed elements of the divine. Stories circulate about statues that suddenly sprang to life, gave prophecies and allowed the gods to speak.

These metopes are appropriate boundary markers. Having passed the halfway mark in the labours, as Alexander points out, we are witnessing Hercules' transition to divinity. One of the ways in which ancient Greek artists differentiated gods from mortals was through scale. Gods were literally larger than life. We can see this in the pedimental sculpture of the temple. Zeus and Apollo, in the centre of each pediment, tower over the surrounding figures.

This superiority in size flowed down the hierarchical chain. As a result heroes were always considered to be larger than ordinary mortals. For example, Plutarch records a story about the fifth-century BC politician and general Cimon, who was given a prophecy by the Delphic oracle that he should bring back the bones of Athens' favourite hero, Theseus, from the island of Scyros to the city for reburial. Following his victory over the island, Cimon sought the bones, but was unable to find them until one day he saw an eagle digging in the dirt. He started to dig in the same spot and moments later discovered some bones whose tremendous size meant that they must belong to Theseus. Even discounting the many fantastic elements of this story, the fact remains that people believed that size and heroism went together. The bones Cimon brought back certainly impressed and convinced people; they even erected a monument in the centre of the city to house them. And Theseus' bones were not the only hero bones in circulation. There are reports of discoveries of similarly impressive bones of heroes throughout the Greek world. Judging by the bones of Orestes found in Tegea, he stood ten feet tall. Quite what these bones came from has puzzled scholars. Some even suggest that they were the fossilised remains of prehistoric animals.

It is striking then that the metopes eschew this game of scale. In the very centre of the tableau that they offer we see Hercules framed by Athena on one side and the titan Atlas on the other. As they crowd the slab, we are reminded about issues of size. Yet no concession is made for Hercules' mortal or heroic status. He stands equal to the gods.

To understand how Hercules could stand toe to toe with the largest titan in the world, we need to begin on the north side of the temple with the Cretan bull. Bulls and Crete go together. Arthur Evans cemented this relationship with his discovery, aided by a large amount of creative thinking, of the bull-leaping, horn-worshipping culture of Minoan Crete. Even before this, or rather instrumental in fuelling Evans' fantasies, was the strong mythic association between bulls and Crete. Two famous bulls feature in Cretan myth. The first was the one that Zeus sent to abduct one of his seemingly endless loves, the beautiful Phoenician princess Europa. Once she was safely on its back, the bull headed out to sea, not stopping until it arrived on Crete, an island conveniently far enough away from parental supervision to allow Zeus to enjoy Europa's company without interruption.

The other famous bull was the one sent by Poseidon (Lat. Neptune) to King Minos of Crete. Minos had promised to sacrifice to Poseidon whatever gift he sent from the sea. Unfortunately, when Poseidon sent a bull of exceptional fineness, Minos decided to keep it and substitute it in the sacrifice with a lesser bull from his own herd. This seems particularly mean when one remembers that in a Greek sacrifice, the gods were offered not the choice cuts of meat, but just the shin wrapped in a bit of skin and fat. It was mortals who really enjoyed the benefits of ancient sacrifice. They received the best cuts. Indeed, for many of them, it was one of the few times they were able to eat meat. Most of the time, for the majority of the Greek population, their diet was largely vegetarian.

Needless to say, Poseidon engineered a suitable revenge. He inspired such lust for the bull in the heart of Minos' wife that she secretly arranged for Minos' chief craftsman, Daedalus, to construct an artificial heifer in which she could lie so that the bull might be lured into mounting her and so satisfy her desire. It worked like a charm, and nine months later the birth of the Minotaur testified to its effectiveness. (Although famous in antiquity, this contraption for the facilitation of insemination has tended, for obvious reasons, to be glossed over in modern lists of Daedalus' most famous inventions in favour of the labyrinth and the wax wings for his son, Icarus.)

Given this surfeit of beef, it is understandable that our sources are unclear which bull was causing the problems on Crete and which one Hercules wrestled to submission and brought back to Eurystheus. All sources are clear that he did not kill the bull. Whichever bull it was, it was divinely sent and killing it risked retribution. Once it had been brought back to Eurystheus, the animal was released, whereupon it apparently wandered off, causing havoc wherever it went. According to an Athenian tradition, it was finally subdued by Theseus on the plains of Marathon (Athens' local hero attempting to muscle in on Hercules' glory).

This labour is balanced on the south side of the temple with the representation of Hercules' taming of the man-eating mares of Diomedes. Flesh rather than grass was their staple. Poets describe how their mouths foamed with the blood of their prey. Once again, it is the female of the species that proves the more deadly and dangerous. It is interesting to note just how many mythological monsters are female. The most famous of these is, of course, the gorgon Medusa – a creature who so effectively combined femininity with the monstrous that she became for Freud the poster-girl for the male fear of female castration, her knotted snakey hair and gnashing teeth a barely repressed representation of the *vagina dentata*. In the course of Hercules' adventures, we have already seen the strange horned hind. Not content with classical depictions of the Stymphalian birds as waterfowl, Western art has always preferred to represent them as harpies. We see these half-women, half-bird creatures not only in Vignon's canvas for Richelieu, but also in perhaps the most influential version of the labour, Albrecht Dürer's *Hercules and the Stymphalian Birds* (c. 1500). Now we have mad flesh-devouring mares. One does not need to go as far as Freud to see male anxiety in all these monstrous females.

Albrecht Dürer, *Hercules and the Stymphalian Birds*. c. 1500.

Appropriately, then, it is Hercules, the paradigm of mas-culinity, who will restore order. The confusion of categories (male/female, carnivore/herbivore) will not be allowed to continue. Taming is what this metope is about. Although it is extremely fragmentary, the most likely reconstruction depicts Hercules bringing the horses under control. One fragment shows his left hand firmly on the bridle. Compositionally, the arrangement of figures echoes the depiction of Hercules wrestling the Cretan bull: his body crosses that of the animal. Importantly, the display is less dynamic than its counterpart. The fight has largely gone out of the animal.

These animals were the property of King Diomedes of Thrace. If bulls have become synonymous with Crete, then the emblematic animal of Thrace is the horse. The Thracians were even rumoured to suckle their children on horses' milk, allowing them to drink it straight from the teat, an idea appalling to all decent Greeks. In such a barbarous place, training your horses to eat flesh did not seem shocking or even surprising. Sources differ on the precise method by which Hercules was able to train the horses. The most poetic describes how the animals became docile once he fed their owner, King Diomedes, to them.

Issues of gender and barbarism are also important in the next labour of Hercules, his quest to retrieve the girdle of the Amazon queen, Hippolyta, which had been given to her by Ares as a sign of her superiority. That Eurystheus' daughter asked her father to obtain it for her merely underscores the unworthiness of this family to rule.

Amazons enjoyed a rich and varied life in Greek imagination. The notion of societies dominated by women fascinated the Greeks. They played with the idea in a number of their comedies and commemorated stories about the Amazons in their literature and art, each tale competing with the next in outrageousness. Rumours circulated about the sexual voraciousness of Amazons, their brutality, and their treatment of men. Sometimes these portrayals were incompatible. So, for example, the story of Amazons removing a breast to assist in archery or javelin-throwing sits at odds with the numerous images of Amazons bare-chested with their perfectly formed, unmutilated breasts proudly displayed.

The obvious erotic pleasure these depictions offer to the viewer tells us something else about the Greek attitude to Amazons. As is often the case, revulsion mixes strongly with desire. This paradigm is established in one of the canonical images from another encounter between Greeks and Amazons. The setting is the plains of Troy, and on a sixth-century BC amphora, now in the British Museum, we see Achilles, his eyes locked on the Amazon queen Penthesileia, as she slumps dying to the ground, felled by his spear. The eyes say it all. It is a look of death and desire. It is an inverse of the poetic truth of Wilde's *The Ballad of Reading Gaol*. Here every man loves the thing he kills.

This strange concoction of passion and disgust is the recipe for the abject, the figures who crystallise a society's fears. Here the fear is the obvious one that every misogynist culture possesses, namely, that male superiority over women, a distinction that they spend so much time portraying as a distinction in nature, might actually be one created by culture. Amazonian culture represents a dangerous, seductive break in the natural order. Needless to say, the Greeks advocated violence as the best response.

Athens was proud to boast that it had once seen off an invasion of Amazons. It became a cliché of the eulogies given over the war dead to remind the mourners of this heroic deed of the past, and to place the actions of the recently deceased in this glorious tradition. The Parthenon commemorated the event twice, once on the outside in a series of metopes. These were paired with a complementary set of images depicting the battle between Lapiths and centaurs which just served to reinforce the Amazons' unnatural status. Which is more freakish – half-men, half-horses or women able to carry weapons? The viewer is left to decide. The other depiction was on the shield of the gold and ivory statue of Athena inside the temple. Here Athena the virgin repudiates her femininity.

Hercules' campaign to retrieve the girdle is stitched together from a number of stories. One of the identifiable genres in classical literature is the epic sea voyage. The paradigm is the *Odyssey*, the story of Odysseus' return to Ithaca. However, Jason's voyage on the *Argo* to retrieve the Golden Fleece, a journey on which Hercules was a brief passenger, rivals it in significance. Hercules' voyage to the land of the Amazons has left less of a trace in literature, but it shares a number of features with these other epics. It likewise consists of a number of individual episodes strung together by an overarching purpose. Numerous places along the way claim to play a part in this adventure and write it into their own myth-histories. The Greek community of Thasos, for example, rested their claims for the ownership of their island on the story that Hercules gave it to them when he stopped there during his travels. Everywhere Hercules touches down he leaves an impression. In his wake, new cities are founded, land is redistributed, heroes are defeated and brigands are brought to justice.

Among all these adventures, there is one that will have important consequences for Hercules' future. It occurs at Troy where, on his arrival, Hercules finds the daughter of the king chained to a rock and being offered to an approaching sea monster. We learn a lot about ancient heroics and the modernity of chivalry when we see that Hercules refuses to lend a hand until he has struck a bargain with the king. In return for rescuing this 'damsel in distress' Hercules demands the king's fine set of horses. These horses were given to the king as compensation for Zeus being allowed to abduct the king's son, Ganymede, to serve as his lover and cup-bearer. Despite these somewhat unfortunate associations, the king welshes on the deal and refuses to hand over the animals. Hercules is furious, but impelled by the necessity of his labour, he is forced to depart before he can exact retribution. He leaves, promising darkly that he will return to wage his own Trojan War.

The other element that this adventure shares with other voyage epics is the way in which the story dramatises the difficulties, dangers and opportunities for miscommunication in dealing with non-Greeks. Initially Hercules' negotiations with Hippolyta go well. She is prepared to hand over her girdle. It is only when Hera intervenes and tells the Amazons that Hercules is planning to abduct their queen that their sudden arrival with spears leads an overly suspicious Hercules to suspect a trap and slay Hippolyta before retreating with the girdle. This is the moment that is captured in the metope. In its focus on the violent acquisition of the girdle, the metope makes a point not only about gender, but also about the inevitable difficulties of communication with 'the other'. Hercules and the Amazon are looking at each other, but there is no understanding.

This failure is especially poignant given the often marginal status that Hercules himself enjoyed. Even his dress served to mark him out as an outsider. The lion skin and club have become such trademarks that we miss how this outfit struck Greek eyes. To the Greeks, Hercules looked like an outlaw, a brigand, a wild man. In the ancient world, one author was blamed for starting this trend – the sixth-century BC poet Stesichorus.

Like the metopes of Zeus at Olympia, Stesichorus' opus exists only in fragments. His works consist of quotations preserved in other writers and a few scraps of papyri dug out of the sands of Egypt. One of his most influential works concerns the next labour of Hercules, his seizure of the cattle from Geryon, a three-headed giant (in some depictions he is even shown with three bodies attached like conjoined triplets). We can judge the popularity of this work not only from the number of people who cite it, but also from an explosion in the images of Geryon that occur on Greek vases in the decades after its publication. All the signs are that this work was a hit.

Labours in Far-off Lands

It is appropriate that Stesichorus should have developed the outlaw outfit for Hercules because this labour is really nothing more than cattle-rustling. Just the sort of bandit behaviour one might expect from someone who goes around in a lion skin armed with a club, although like most serious crime it does have its glamorous side. Hercules joins a distinguished line of cattle thieves. One of the stories told about the infant god Hermes was that he stole the cattle of Apollo, making them walk backwards to obscure their tracks.

Again we find Hercules having to undertake a long journey with all its attendant adventures. Monsters are completely cleared from Libya and Crete. He even attacks the Sun for beating down too hard on him, firing his poisoned arrows at the god until the Sun placates him by giving him a giant golden goblet in which he is able to float to Geryon's island. The idea of such a giant cup was certainly popular with the drinking crowd, who loved retelling the story at their symposiums. This episode forms the subject of a witty fifth-century BC Greek drinking cup which shows Hercules bobbing up and down in a giant goblet. Painted on the inside of the cup, the image is revealed only when the contents are drained and the inebriated viewer has begun to understand what it might be like to be trapped inside a giant cup, at the mercy of a wine-dark sea. Drunkenness and seasickness seem to go together in the Greek mind; one ancient author preserves a story about a party where matters got so out of hand that guests in their drunken delirium imagined that they were trapped on a sinking ship and ended up throwing furniture out of the window to lighten the load.

His passage alters Europe's relationship with Africa. Previously the two continents had been joined together by an isthmus that separated the Mediterranean from the Atlantic Ocean. To assist his journey Hercules sundered the connection, digging a strait through the isthmus. To celebrate this achievement, he erected a pillar on either side of the strait: one on Gibraltar, the other on the African coast on the rock of Abyla. Symbolically then, Hercules is responsible for separating Africa from Europe. When Hercules cuts, he cuts deep. The conceptual division that he sets up plays an important part in the subsequent European history of colonialism, genocide and enslavement of the African continent.

After all these adventures, Hercules' encounter with Geryon risks being an anti-climax. The metope at Olympia gets around this by making Geryon as monstrous as possible. He is shown here dominating the space of the metope. One head is dead, but two still fight on.

The metope chooses one path, Stesichorus chose another. His genius lay in making Geryon not monstrous, but human. In a passage full of pathos, Geryon meditates on the value of life and death as he goes out to meet his doom at the hands of Hercules. Hercules does not take him in a clean fight. Instead, he relies on stealth and trickery. Like a sniper, he creeps up on his opponent before firing one of his envenomed arrows into the monster's forehead. In one of the most singular and beautiful images from Greek poetry, Stesichorus describes how Geryon's head falls as 'the poppy droops, its petals blown'.

Having obtained the cattle from their monstrous guardian, Hercules begins the arduous task of herding them back to Greece. It is a journey that proves even more eventful than the one that brought him to Geryon's island. On his return, he passes through Spain, France and Italy, and finally reaches Greece. Apart from a quick dalliance with a snake-woman in Scythia, it is his time in Italy that proves most fraught. We get a glimpse of one of his adventures here in a painting by Dominiquin, *Landscape with Hercules and Cacus* (1621).

The painting now hangs in the Louvre, rushed past by numerous tourists as they queue to see the *Mona Lisa*. It shows a bucolic landscape of mountains, lakes and streams. Ostensibly the subject is Hercules' defeat of the giant Cacus, who, using the same ruse as the infant Hermes of dragging them back by the tail, managed to steal the cattle of Geryon from Hercules while he slept. The painting shows Hercules emerging from Cacus' cave on the Avertine hill, one of the seven hills of Rome. Here he tracked down the giant, slew him, and retrieved his cattle. However, all these events in Dominiquin's canvas are sidelined in favour of the landscape in which they occur. It is its features – the lakes, the streams, the mountains, the spectacular sky – that the viewer is supposed to enjoy. Hercules is a tiny figure in the corner. One has to search to find him. The hero receives exactly the same treatment in a canvas by Poussin (*Landscape with Hercules and Cacus*) in the Pushkin museum in Moscow. These works echo an important truth about the stories concerning the return of Geryon's cattle. Deep down they are really just an excuse for exploring Italy.

Italy – even its name holds associations with Hercules' cattle drive. According to ancient Greek lexicographers, the word derives from *italos* 'a bull' and gave rise to the name of the region because this was where one of Hercules' cattle, breaking free, roamed until he could recapture it. A variant on this story explains that for this reason the area also used to be called Vitulia (from the Latin *vitulus* 'a calf'). The journey of Hercules and the cattle of Geryon came to occupy an important place in the myth-history of Rome. He was responsible for dividing up various parts of the city. He provides the explanation for all sorts of anomalies in Roman religious practice. It was he who set up the altar to Saturn by the hill from the Forum to the Capitol, and it is for this reason that the sacrifice there was performed in 'a Greek fashion'. He abolished human sacrifice, replacing it with the practice of throwing effigies into the Tiber. It was in Italy that Hercules first received sacrifices as a god (Athens, of course, disputes this). The altar on which this act occurred was known as the *Ara maxima*, 'The Greatest Altar'. It stood in Rome, appropriately enough, near the cattle markets. Women were forbidden from its rites, a fact that was justified on the grounds that Hercules had found himself similarly excluded by Roman women when they were celebrating the all-female festival, the *Bona Dea*.

The next labour brings us to one of the best preserved of the metopes. This concerns Hercules' expedition to retrieve the apples of the Hesperides. These golden apples had been a wedding gift from the Earth goddess to Hera to celebrate her marriage to Zeus. To protect them, Hera had established them in a garden at the end of the world where they were guarded by a giant serpent. The garden was tended by the daughters of Atlas, the Hesperides.

Hercules' first problem lay in determining the location of the apples. This information could be obtained only from the sea god Nereus, who refused to divulge it until Hercules wrestled it out of him. During this combat Nereus attempted to evade Hercules' grip by constantly changing shape. However, Hercules held fast and an exhausted Nereus relented and revealed where the apples were to be found. The combat between Nereus and Hercules mimics another more famous battle with a shape-shifter, that between Menelaus and Proteus. The story is essentially the same. Lost in Egypt after the end of the Trojan War, the hero Menelaus learns how to get home by wrestling the information out of the shape-shifting sea god Proteus. No matter how dangerous or slippery a form his opponent adopted, Menelaus held firm until, realising the futility of further struggle, Proteus agreed to provide all the crucial information to ensure a safe passage to Sparta. The idea of shape-shifting is a popular one in classical literature. Ovid had no trouble collecting dozens of such stories in his *Metamorphoses*. In a culture where everybody in public life was constantly playing different roles, adopting a different *persona* (Latin 'a mask') for various audiences, the appeal of such transformations is obvious.

Nereus' advice takes Hercules on another long journey. In Libya, he wrestles with Antaeus, the son of Earth, whom Hercules is unable to defeat until he realises that Antaeus is invincible only while his feet have contact with his mother.

Once he is held aloft, Antaeus' strength disappears, and Hercules crushes him with ease. In Egypt, he is captured by King Busiris, who attempts to sacrifice the hero to the Egyptian gods. As he is dragged to the altar, Hercules bursts his bonds and then slays the king. Having developed a taste for regicide, he continues on his journey, stopping to kill Emathion, the king of Ethiopia.

It is all too easy to read Greek prejudice and fear about the outside world into these tales. They seem to confirm a worldview that outside Greece the world is strange and barbaric. Certainly, they could be used to make this point. The story of Busiris features in a number of xenophobic vase-paintings where Hercules battles Busiris and his Egyptian henchmen. These images are detailed studies in ethnic difference. Hercules stands tall, proud and muscled; the Egyptians, fat and soft and with shaved heads, cower before him. No opportunity for pointing out differences in custom is lost. We even get details such as the phalluses of the Egyptians being shown as circumcised, a practice the Greeks found strange and absurd.

However, alongside this strain of xenophobia in Greek thought, there also existed an open-minded, cosmopolitan attitude that was receptive to new ideas and experiments. So, for example, we find the historian Herodotus called a 'barbarian-lover' because his history of Greco-Persian wars refused to be a piece of crude jingoism. Instead, he shows a sympathy for the different cultures of the Mediterranean and a desire to understand their ways. Sometimes his own cultural prejudices mean that this project fails. At other times, he is more successful. The story of Busiris is a touchstone for his tolerance. He is not prepared to accept such tales and berates his contemporaries for repeating them. In giving his account of Egypt, he denies that such events could have occurred. Egyptian religion, he declares, was totally opposed to the concept of human sacrifice. The story is riddled with holes, and he suggests that it should be rejected.

The metope at Olympia brings us to the culmination of this labour. Here we see Hercules receiving the apples from Atlas. They have disappeared from one of Atlas' hands, but are clearly visible in the other. Hercules provides the central vertical in the composition. It needs to be a strong vertical; he is supporting the heavens. In order to avoid the dangers of the serpent, Hercules sent Atlas, the father of the Hesperides, to retrieve the apples. Doing so required Hercules to release Atlas from his usual burden of supporting the heavens on his shoulders. As always Athena is present to give a helping hand. She balances the composition on the left-hand side. Moreover, she is there to ensure a smooth transition between Atlas and Hercules. In some versions of the story, Atlas is reluctant to resume his burden when he returns with the apples and does so only after being tricked by Hercules into agreeing to hold the sky up for a few moments while Hercules finds a cushion for his neck.

However, it need not have happened this way. An alternative version of the myth omits the Atlas episode and has Hercules defeating the guardian serpent with his arrows before going to retrieve the apples himself. This version seems to have been the inspiration for a marvellous automaton mentioned by the first-century AD inventor Hero of Alexandria. The machine recreated the garden of the Hesperides, complete with apple tree, serpent and thieving Hercules. The onlooker was invited to pick one of the apples for himself. In doing so, he triggered a mechanism which brought the machine to life. The serpent began to hiss and Hercules drew back his bow. Such machines were typical of the technological marvels of the Hellenistic period. The courts of Alexander's successors enjoyed water-organs, temple doors that automatically opened as if by magic, fully automated puppet theatres, and robotic doves that flew through the air powered by steam. One thing that has puzzled scholars is why such technological sophistication and expertise never translated into a full-blown industrial revolution. The answer seems to lie in mindset. Why turn your attention to industry when you have the most perfect robot working for you already, the slave? Given the structure of the Hellenistic world, it was more profitable to design marvellous machines that improved your standing at court than to produce one that could spin wool faster.

In choosing to feature the story of Hercules supporting the heavens in this metope, the sculptures foreground the issue of Hercules' tremendous strength. It takes a lot of muscles to hold up the sky, a fact which we can see demonstrated by the Farnese Hercules. This statue is a Roman copy of a Hellenistic original. Although a number of such copies survive, this is the most impressive. The piece is named after its most illustrious owners, the Farnese family, in whose affections, as we have already seen, Hercules occupied a particular place. The statue is a masterpiece of musculature. Hercules ripples and bulges from every angle. And every angle is what the piece demands that you appreciate. Like Hero's automaton, it wants to have

Lysippus, *Weary Hercules* ('The Farnese Hercules').
Roman copy after Greek original.

some fun with the Hesperides story. By means of a cheap trick, it draws your eyes around itself. From the front, it is clear that Hercules is coyly hiding something behind his back.

Forced to walk round, inevitably noting the muscles on the way, the viewer discovers that the prize which Hercules has secreted in his hands is nothing other than the apples of the Hesperides.

Having now travelled everywhere in the known world, there is only one place for Hercules to go, and that is the Underworld. His final task was to bring Eurystheus the three-headed hound Cerberus from the Underworld. A descent into the Underworld is something every hero has to make. Orpheus, Odysseus, Aeneas all made the journey. There is even a Greek word for the trip, *katabasis* 'going under'. It becomes such a stock item that the Athenian comic playwright Aristophanes even parodies it. In his *Frogs*, he sends Dionysus, played as a snivelling coward, into the Underworld. Unsure about the route and its dangers, Dionysus is forced to ask Hercules for advice.

Such guidance was often sought. In the ancient world there was no end of magicians, cults, and religious mysteries which promised beneficial advice about the afterlife. Death was not something that simply happened, it needed mediation. Even Hercules participated in the Eleusinian mysteries, one of the most popular mysteries cults, prior to his descent into the Underworld. Getting to the Underworld alive was a difficult business. Dead, of course, it was no problem. Certain places in the Mediterranean became known as entrances. Two places were identified in the ancient world as the site of Hercules' descent, Taenarum in the Peloponnese and Heracleia Pontica on the Black Sea. Both were important sites in the ancient world for necromancy, places where the living and the dead could communicate.

His guide for his visit to the Underworld is the god Hermes, who points out many of the spirits they pass on their way. These include the gorgon Medusa and the hero Meleager. Hermes has a number of associations with the Underworld. He conducted the souls of the dead there. Magic spells often invoke him. A common method of cursing someone in the ancient world was to write a letter on lead to Hermes asking him to bring harm to a victim. These lead letters were then 'posted' into a well or grave. Archaeologists have found hundreds of them.

Hermes is present in the metope at Olympia, but only just. We can see a few fragments of his foot on the right-hand side of the slab. The rest of the metope is dominated by Hercules straining on a leash as he drags Cerberus into the daylight. It is proving quite a struggle. Concentration is written all over Hercules' face as he reels in Cerberus like a prize game fish. According to one tradition, Cerberus was so afraid of daylight that when he first encountered it, he threw up over the aconite plant, turning it from an innocuous herb into a deadly poisonous one.

However, it is not just Cerberus that Hercules brought back from the Underworld. According to a number of accounts, he rescued Theseus as well. It was Theseus' gratitude for this action that prompted him to offer his assistance to the maddened Hercules in Euripides' *Heracles*. Indeed, rescuing people from Death becomes part of Hercules' routine. So, for example, Alcestis, who selflessly offers herself up to Death in place of her husband – the rest of his family, including his elderly parents, having passed up the opportunity to make such a noble sacrifice – finds herself rescued from this fate by the arrival on the scene of a drunk Hercules. Tipsy and unable to understand why everyone seems so glum, he feels suitably admonished when events are explained to him. As penance for his thoughtlessness, he wrestles Death and wins back the queen's life.

With the conquering of Death, we complete our circuit of the temple of Zeus and can begin to think about the totality of the labours. Paradoxically, they are both less and more than the sum of their parts. To get a greater sense of the value of this unity, it helps if we focus on the Greek term for the labours. The word 'labour' is derived from the Latin term meaning *toil* or *exertion*. In Greek, the word used for each labour is *athlon* 'contest'. It is the word that lies behind the names for modern sporting events such as the triathlon, pentathlon, heptathlon and decathlon. The prefix changes to indicate the number of events in each contest (i.e. 3, 5, 7, 10).

There is something of this sporting logic about Hercules' labours. As in the decathlon, sometimes the most impressive aspect is cumulative success across a range of activities rather than performance in any individual event. So it is with the 'Twelve Labours'. They come to be appreciated more as a unit than as a series of individual events. Indeed, some individual labours often fall out of the public consciousness. A survey of depictions of the labours from the medieval period onwards reveals remarkable unevenness in the portrayal of individual labours. For artists, it seems that the 'Twelve Labours of Hercules' is really 'The Lion, the Hydra and ten others'. Indeed, it is hard to eradicate the suspicion that part of the success of the motif of the 'Twelve Labours' lies in the fact that the number twelve, with its easy divisibility (12:2, 12:3, 12:4, 12:6), makes an ideal basis for a decorative programme. With this sort of symmetry it is easy to cover anything from a Roman sarcophagus to the walls of an Italian palazzo. Certainly, the ease of division is one of the features that writers of handbooks on symbolic imagery in decoration give as one of the reasons in favour of adopting the labours as a decorative scheme.

Of course, it is not just mathematics. Local interest makes a difference. We have seen how the labour involving the cattle of Geryon occupied a particularly important place in the Roman mindset. Similarly the labour of the Augean stables resonated more strongly at Olympia than anywhere else in Greece. We can imagine the same process happening all over the Mediterranean as individual communities gave their own spin to the labours of Hercules, each city-state and community adopting, adapting and supplementing this pan-Hellenic storyline for its own purposes. Nor did this process stop with the end of the classical world. Modern France became attached to its own peculiar Gallic Hercules. Hercules' activities become useful for explaining customs ('Why aren't there any women at the *Ara maxima*?'), natural phenomena ('Why is aconite so poisonous?', 'Why do the waters of the Anigrus smell?') and the unknown ('What lies at the far west of the Mediterranean?').

However, perhaps the strongest force that has kept numerous artists and intellectuals returning to the labours is their allegorical potential. From the Greeks onwards we see

The Hercules of the Union, Slaying the Great Dragon of Secession.
Civil war cartoon, 1861.

a desire for each labour to tell a story that is bigger than just an action sequence with a happy ending. These labours have

grown to encompass most of human experience. Reform
against corruption and the cleansing of the Augean stables
have become wedded together. One could easily write a
long history on the use of the hydra as a political metaphor.
This book opened with just such a usage during the time of
the French Revolution. Nor were those revolutionaries
taking a risk in using the hydra in this way. There was already
a long-established tradition of such allegorical hydras. Even
in the time of Henri IV of France, the hydra's potential was
being explored. We possess both a painting and a proposal
for a monument in which Henri crushes a hydra representing the forces of anarchy and political dissent. However, it is
in its appearance in more modern political imagery that we
see its usefulness best. The hydra works well because it allows
us to understand phenomena that would otherwise be
incomprehensible or difficult to articulate. Through its many
heads we can connect disparate forces arrayed against us. It
allows us to represent the way in which seemingly inde-
pendent events can be interrelated. We see this in political
cartoons where each head represents a different problem
(poor health, wages, high crime, etc.) all stemming from the
same cause. The hydra allows us to begin to analyse and
critique institutions. The hydra allows the beginning of
political theory.

CHAPTER SIX

Death and Apotheosis

What happens when an irresistible force meets an immovable object? We find this paradoxical situation represented on the leg of a bronze tripod from Olympia. It depicts two figures wrestling over a tripod. The struggle is evenly matched. Neither party shows any signs of giving way. They look to be trapped for eternity in this struggle. This motif of 'the tripod wrestlers' seems to be a popular one. Judging by the design of the helmets worn by the protagonists, it may even originate in the Near East. While it is not possible to identify the two figures in the early versions of this struggle, it does not take long for identities to be grafted on to this motif. The struggle over the tripod is traditionally depicted as a struggle between Hercules and Apollo. The action is set in Delphi. Hercules has seized the tripod, one of the symbols of the Delphic oracle, and has decided to cart it off and set up his own oracle. Apollo intervenes and attempts to wrestle the tripod back. It is a struggle which threatens to upset the divine order. In the conflict between Apollo and

Hercules and Apollo Wrestle Over the Delphic Tripod. Terracotta relief from the sanctuary of Apollo on the Palatine. First century BC.

Hercules, who should win? We'll never know. In order to prevent a resolution (or perhaps to effect one), Zeus hurls a thunderbolt and parts the quarrelling pair, thus avoiding the conflict between divine force and stasis.

This is the second time in the cycle of Hercules stories that Zeus has needed to intervene to preserve his investment in the logical ordering of the cosmos. The first time occurred during Amphitryon's campaign against the Teleboans to avenge the murder of Alcmena's brothers. To assist him in his campaign, Amphitryon attempted to enlist the help of Creon of Thebes. Creon agreed to join Amphitryon, but on the condition that Amphitryon first rid Thebes of a vixen (yet another monstrous female) that had been harassing the flocks and causing general havoc. Prophecy had foretold that this vixen was destined never to be caught. Amphitryon's solution to the problem is inspired – he enlists the help of a dog which was fated to catch whatever it pursued. Once again the paradox forces Zeus' hand, and he is obliged to turn both animals to stone.

There was a ready market for such paradoxes among the Greeks. In the public spaces of most ancient cities, we find teachers delivering virtuoso displays of rhetoric and logic for their eager customers. The relationship between nature and culture, the composition of the cosmos, the physiognomy of the gods, and the processes of human life were all favourite topics. These performances often had an adversarial edge to them as rival teachers sought to outwit and show up their competitors. It is this dialectical aspect that explains a number of distinctive features about the nature and history of Greek philosophy. In such an environment, it is inevitable that arguments are ruthlessly pursued to their logical, and often illogical, conclusion and old debates are constantly revisited from a new angle. It is not surprising that the 'dialogue' format turned out to be one of the most distinctive and influential features of Greek philosophy. Philosophy was a constant conversation. Even when philosophers are making their most dogmatic and imperious pronouncements, they do so with an eye to an unvoiced opposition. Trapping an opponent in an apparent paradox was a regular stratagem in these games of intellectual brinkmanship.

We get a taste of such exchanges in the numerous stories which surround a pair of Sicilian rhetoricians – the teacher Corax and his former student Tisias. Tisias' constant attempts to upstage and outwit his former instructor are the subject of a number of anecdotes. Despite this rivalry, it was not an entirely destructive relationship. As a by-product of this feuding, the pair also accidentally laid down the rules for the science of rhetoric. One of the most famous exchanges between them occurred when Corax tried to sue Tisias to recover the fees that the latter owed him for Corax's lessons in rhetoric. Unfortunately for Corax, matters go awry when the case arrives in court. In his defence, Tisias argues that if he cannot persuade the jury of his case, then the rhetorical instruction that he has received from Corax was worthless, and so he need not pay. Conversely, if he can persuade the jury of the rightness of his case, he wins the case and does not have to pay. In either case, the consequence of each premise is that Tisias avoids his debts. Although almost certainly fictional, these stories establish an important paradigm for philosophic exchange.

While on one level this tripod motif sends us towards philosophy, at the same time it also prompts us to think about the nature of competition. It is appropriate that the struggle between Apollo and Hercules should concern a tripod. These were the Greek prizes *par excellence*. These three-legged multi-functional cauldrons are one of the most important and earliest features of Greek material culture. They make regular appearances in the archaeological record from the eighth century onwards. The Pythia, the priestess of Apollo, would sit on a tripod when she gave her oracular pronouncements. Yet their more common appearance was as prizes for competitions and dedications at sanctuaries by grateful victors. One of our earliest literary references relates to the tripods won at the funeral games for Patroclus that were later set up as dedications to the spirits of the dead heroes. In Athens, the winners of the dithyrambic competition were awarded bronze tripods by the city. These tripods were massive affairs, up to five metres in height and costing about two years' wages. Victors would often erect these tripods near the theatre and sanctuary of Dionysus. They formed such a distinctive feature of the Athenian civic landscape that they gave their name to a road that ran through them, *Tripodes* (Tripods Street). This name still exists today for the street that goes from the Plaka towards the theatre of Dionysus. Tripods attracted their own historian. Among the lost works from antiquity is the treatise by the second-century BC Athenian historian Heliodorus entitled 'On the Tripods of Athens'. There was even a genre of song developed to accompany the processions of tripods through the city. Perhaps the most distinguished surviving example of these victory monuments is that to Lysicrates. Erected to

Hercules

celebrate Lysicrates' victory in 335–4 BC in the boys' dithyrambic competition, it has attracted admiration throughout the centuries. Lord Elgin wanted to acquire it in addition to his plundered marbles. The architects James Stuart and Nicholas Revett gave it prominence in their famous eighteenth-century work *The Antiquities of Athens*. This brought it to even greater attention and inspired a number of copies. Replicas of this monument can be found as far afield as Calton Hill in Edinburgh and the Botanic Gardens of Sydney.

It is hard not to see an allusion to this competitive dimension in the 'struggle for the tripod' motif. This seems to be the case in the Olympia tripod where the motif, placed as it is on the leg of the tripod, reminds us that struggle supports such valued prizes. The battle between Hercules and Apollo teaches the viewer that tripods are hard won and that ultimately their distribution lies in the hands of the most powerful of the gods.

Finally, in addition to being a story about tripods, this competition is also a tale of impiety, murder and hubris. Hercules stole the tripod only because the priestess was refusing to grant his request for purification. He seems to have exhausted the patience of the oracle. There was only so much blood that could be washed away. The process by which Hercules had once again found himself infected by the miasma of murder is convoluted and disputed. The victim in every account remains the same, the Oechalian prince, Iphitus. Hercules had fallen out with this royal household during his search for a bride after the completion of his labours. His

desired conquest was Iole, the daughter of the King of
Oechalia, Eurytus. She was the prize in an archery competition
between potential suitors and the king and his sons. It is a
story which shares a number of similarities with that of Pelops
and Oinomaus, in particular, the central figure of the daughter
who can be acquired only by besting the father in competition.
Anthropologists and Freudians love such stories because their
essential elements (the traffic in women, the father–daughter
relationship) seem to conform to the underlying structures
that they postulate for society. Myth may well spring from
such dark recesses. However, what such explanations cannot
account for are the surface details that give these stories their
distinctive colour (why archery as opposed to chariot-racing?).
They have trouble explaining mythic variation. Moreover, in
unifying them into one central ur-narrative, it is easy to miss
the way that some stories critique and subvert dominant
narratives.

When Hercules comes forward to receive his prize, the
family refuses to hand over Iole. Hercules is the last person
that parents could desire as a son-in-law. A dangerous, violent outsider with the blood of his first wife and children on
his hands, what guarantee does he offer for the safe continuation of their line? What Hercules demonstrates is the
ridiculousness of such competitions as a method for determining suitable marriage stock. If you wish to rest your
genetic future on the flight of an arrow then by all means do
so; just be prepared to have someone like Hercules joining
you at the family meal table.

According to some traditions, the only person who

argued against the family's decision was Eurytus' son, Iphitus. At some point soon after, Hercules murdered him. Some accounts say that Hercules went mad and threw Iphitus from a wall after feasting with his newfound friend. Others say that, in his rage at being denied the hand of Iole, Hercules stole livestock from Eurytus and that, when Iphitus tried to retrieve it, Hercules murdered him. In any case, even the most charitable interpretations of Hercules' actions cannot excuse his behaviour at Delphi. In seizing the tripod and seeking to found his own oracle, one which would give him the answers he wanted, he deliberately insulted Apollo. It was only natural that Apollo would spring to his oracle's defence. Hercules' actions transgress a number of the most important prohibitions in the Greek mind.

The theft of temple property was a serious crime for the Greeks. It even warranted a special term, *hierosulia*. As one of the major repositories of wealth, temples were one of the prime targets for crime and they were protected by the most extreme sanctions. At Athens, theft of temple property was one of the few crimes where, if the criminal was caught in the act, they could be punished by summary execution. Individuals who stole the property of Delphi met with similar punishment. One of the most famous victims of this tough justice was the fable-writer Aesop. According to a fictional biography, he was framed by a number of Delphic citizens, who felt wounded by some of the sharp barbs in his fables. They planted some ritual gold vessels in his luggage. As he was leaving Delphi, his property was searched and the vessels were discovered. Despite his protestations of innocence, the poor writer was found guilty and thrown to his death from one of the many cliffs around this site.

It was not just individuals who were attracted to the wealth of these sanctuaries. Ambitious city-states were also keen to get their hands on the loot. Interference with Delphi by different city-states provoked at least three 'Sacred Wars' with outraged cities rising up to crusade against such impiety. The war that is best attested historically occurred in the fourth century BC when Phocis seized Delphi. Numerous Greek city-states banded together to dislodge it. Eventually success was achieved by Philip of Macedon who, on the back of his victory and its accompanying prestige, was able to consolidate his position in Greece and so lay the ground-work for the subsequent Macedonian domination of the Greek world by himself and his son, Alexander the Great. As Hercules is made to realise, you set powerful forces in motion when you mess with Delphi.

It is not just through his theft of property that Hercules commits a serious transgression. His actions confuse categories such as public and private religion. The idea of a personal oracle is absurd. It demonstrates a level of pride and ambition that verges on the obscene. Hercules is setting himself up as a figure to rival the gods. A brake needs to be put on his ascent to divinity, and Zeus and Apollo devise a suitable punishment for his crimes. Hercules is sold into slavery for three years. The money which he fetches at auction is to be paid to the family of Iphitus as a blood-debt.

Hercules was bought by Queen Omphale of Lydia, a kingdom in Asia Minor famed for its luxury and indulgence.

The wealth of its most famous ruler, Croesus, has passed into proverb. In Greek musical theory, Lydian music was characterised by the use of a particular mode or scale which the Greeks regarded as soft and effeminate. Everything about the Lydians smacked of wealth and extravagance. According to the Greeks, the Lydians were the first people to develop coinage. These coins were made from electrum, an alloy of gold and silver. A 'Lydian stone' is another name for a touchstone, a variety of black jasper which can be used to tell the fineness and quality of gold.

Hercules is now the slave of a barbarian queen, and his humiliation is compounded by the treatment that he receives at her hands. She strips him of his lion skin, choosing to wear it herself. Dressed in women's clothes, Hercules is forced to perform women's tasks such as spinning and weaving. According to one tradition, he wore one of the queen's jewelled bands as symbol of his subjugation.

The strange dynamic of this relationship is explored in a spectacular canvas by Rubens. The painting was originally commissioned to accompany a depiction of the *Death of Adonis* for the Genovese merchant Giovanni Vincenzo Imperiale. However, it soon caught the well-trained eye of Carlo II Conzaga, Duke of Mantua and famous collector. It shows Hercules at his most humiliated: the queen, standing on a fountain, dominates the hero. Hercules' lion skin hangs draped over her shoulders. This symbol of his triumph in the labours is now nothing more than a plaything for the queen's lapdog which tussles and snaps at the pelt. The queen supports herself with Hercules' club as she leans over to tweak

the ear of the hero. Hercules is forced to spin for the amuse-
ment of a couple of onlooking girls. An elderly female
attendant holds up a shuttle so that Hercules can complete

Peter Paul Rubens, *Hercules and Omphale.* 1602–5.

his weaving tasks. All generations of women conspire in the
hero's downfall. A laughing bust of Pan presides over the
scene.

Only the base of the fountain indicates that there might be more going on here than the humiliation of the hero. It depicts two blind cupids in a chariot. One horse pulls forward while the other horse buckles against the bridle and pulls against the reins. This relief panel alludes to Plato's *Phaedrus*, a dialogue about love and the nature of the soul. It is a typically witty allusion by Rubens, one of the artists best versed in the classical tradition. Already we can feel the presence of the antique world in Hercules' torso which replicates the Belvedere torso, a headless fragment of ancient sculpture beloved by Michelangelo and often identified as coming from a statue of Hercules. However, Rubens' classical learning was not confined merely to ancient art. His elder brother Philip was an accomplished classical scholar who collaborated with Rubens on a book on the dress and customs of the Ancients. The passage from the *Phaedrus* alluded to by this relief comes from the section where Plato enumerates his ideas on the tripartite division of the soul. This he likened to a chariot drawn by a pair of winged horses. One of them is well behaved, the other obstreperous. The charioteer represents Reason, the good horse is noble desire and the bad horse is base passion. Only by Reason keeping the bad one in check can the soul have any hope of ascending to heaven.

In representing blind love unable to control base desire, Rubens adds an erotic charge to this humiliation. He reminds us that Omphale and Hercules were not just mistress and slave, they were also lovers. The kings of Lydia claimed descent from their union. Wealthy Croesus even seems to have inherited his predecessor's inability to deal effectively with the Delphic oracle. When inquiring as to whether he should march against Cyrus and the might of the Persian Empire, he was advised that, should he do so, 'a great empire will fall'. It is only after his subsequent defeat that he learns that this empire was his. There is much for the bust of Pan in this painting to enjoy.

One of the things that Pan mocks is the comedy of sex and gender. Cross-dressing brings this issue to the fore. What makes a man a man? Is it the way one dresses or behaves or does it involve something more essential? The significance of the issue in the Omphale story can be seen in a red-figure Athenian vase. Here the artist deliberately chooses to stop the action at precisely the moment at which Omphale hands over the clothes. We see Hercules reaching out to grab them, he offers his lion skin in return. The significance of this moment was felt even by those scholars who misidentified the scene as one where Hercules receives the poisoned clothes that will cause his death. There is something fatal about these garments. The essentiality of masculinity hangs in the balance. We are left wondering what sort of transformation these clothes will effect. If Hercules, the very paradigm of masculinity, fails this test, what hope is there for the rest of mankind?

As subsequent depictions prove, Hercules passes this test with flying colours. This clothing never manages to restrain him. The dress always looks comic rather than appropriate. Hercules can never 'pass'. This is often the way with heroes, their true gender will always come out. Thetis' attempt to prevent her son Achilles being taken off to the Trojan War by dressing him as a girl was always doomed to failure. Achilles hid among the women of the court, and his disguise initially proved perfect. Odysseus, who was sent to fetch the young man, was unable to locate him. However, wily Odysseus was not to be beaten by such a trick and so he gave a number of trinkets to the 'maidens'. In addition to perfume, mirrors and jewellery, these gifts also included a sword and shield. As they rushed forward to take their gifts, Odysseus arranged for a horn to be sounded in alarm. The women started back in fear. Only Achilles stepped forward to seize the weapons and deal with the immediate danger. One cannot displace or lose one's masculinity.

Or so the Greeks and Romans desperately hoped. For alongside these stories, there existed the very real fear that gender was far more mutable than these tales allowed. Femininity could rub off. Playing women could be a dangerous business. This idea seems to lurk behind part of the ancient prejudice against the acting profession – their ability to play women so effectively aroused suspicion. Routine insults for men were based on ideas of effeminacy and softness. Passive homosexuals were derided not out of homophobia, but because they seemed to be adopting positions more suited to women. Gender needed to be policed.

Nor were these anxieties confined to the classical period. One of the more intriguing chapters in the life of Rubens' painting of Hercules and Omphale is its period as the property of Queen Christina of Sweden. This masterpiece depicting antiquity's most famous cross-dressing moment served as a backdrop for one of history's most famous cross-dressers. Born in 1626, the only child of King Gustaf Adolf II and Queen Maria Eleonora of Brandenburg, Christina became at an extremely early age the sole ruler of one of the most important European powers. Significantly, her reign oversaw the end of the Thirty Years' War. Raised a Protestant, she abdicated the throne when she was received into the Roman Catholic faith in 1654. After her abdication, she lived in exile in Rome in the Palazzo Riario. Throughout her life she remained an enigmatic figure. She never married and numerous lesbian affairs were rumoured. She was passionate in her female friendships, most notably with the beautiful Ebba Sparre. She regularly dressed and acted as a man. In her autobiography, addressed to God, she thanks the Lord for 'not letting any of the defects of my own sex be inherent in my soul, which You in mercy have made altogether male, just as the rest of my being'. Such behaviour and writings prompted speculation that she was a hermaphrodite. Even the exhumation of her bones in 1965 could not put these rumours to rest as the report concluded that her true gender could not be definitively determined. The most it could say was that 'her pelvis had a construction that by itself could not have hindered a delivery'.

To a figure who manipulated and contravened so many of the contemporary rules of female behaviour, the appeal of Rubens' *Hercules and Omphale* is obvious. Moreover, it formed part of a much larger programme of self-representation through art in the Palazzo Riario. Through classical iconography, Christina was able to express herself. Her desire to be viewed as a masculine ruler is confirmed by the constant twinning of herself with Alexander the Great throughout the decoration of the palazzo. Her other iconographic *alter ego* was the virgin Athena, who appears on numerous commemorative medallions. These also allude to the figure of Omphale by having Athena sporting a lion skin. In her Grand Chamber, she prominently displayed, among her fine collection of paintings, a selection of extremely erotic female nudes. These included Correggio's sequence of the loves of Zeus, his paintings of Io, Leda, Danae and Ganymede. When they passed to the Duke of Bracciano these paintings were deemed so carnal that they were displayed behind curtains. Through her art, Christina was consciously refusing to identify herself as a conventional female viewer.

Hercules and Omphale seem to rise to the surface whenever gender roles are under interrogation. If we trace forward the ownership of the Rubens, we find it entering the collection of Philippe of Orleans, the Regent of France after the death of Louis XIV. Here it seems to have influenced the academician Charles-Antoine Coypel in his depiction of this couple. Coypel's painting is just one of a number of important representations of Hercules and Omphale that were produced during the French regency and the early reign of Louis XV. The artists Lemoyne, Dumont and Boucher produced versions. The image spoke to the period in a number of ways. Some saw in it a deliberate reference to the relationship between Louis XV and his mistress Madame de Pompadour. For others, it provided a more general allegory for contemporary gender relations.

Death and Apotheosis

The rise in importance of salon society meant that many aristocrats and their entourages were eschewing battlefield adventures (hanging up their metaphorical clubs) in favour of the pleasures of the boudoir. This was a time in which women were able to exercise control and power in a manner that was previously unthinkable. Omphale represents both the dangers and desires of the age.

The contrast between the various images produced by different artists is striking. In these portrayals, we can see the outlines of contemporary debates and discussions on the topics of gender and power. For example, Coypel warned his viewers about the subjugation of the male. His Hercules is so emasculated that he can barely support a beard. He lies naked at the queen's feet, his modesty preserved only by a cupid which covers his loins with the queen's cloak. The spinning distaff emerges from his side like a spear that has fatally wounded him. Omphale prods him disdainfully with her toe. An attendant cupid gestures towards Hercules as if he were a trussed-up gift.

At the other extreme is a work such as Boucher's painting of the couple. Here all notions of hierarchy have been shed. The signifiers of status, the clothes, lie heaped on the floor. Hercules and Omphale are caught in a most erotic embrace and their naked fleshy forms dominate the painting. Hercules' muscular hand pumps Omphale's right breast. A spray of white fabric issues from his loins and plunges between her thighs. An amazed figure trapped in a roundel behind them can only gesture towards the astonishing scene. Hercules has seized control. He is no longer the slave. The jewelled band which served as a sign of his slavery is now worn by the queen. This painting, shocking in its carnality, sold at auction in 1777 for a staggering 3,840 *livres*, a figure over ten times the estimate.

François Boucher, *Hercules and Omphale*. 1731–4.

However, Hercules' adventures with Omphale were not just confined to the bedroom. Exploits not already allocated to his period of service to Eurystheus are often parked here, during his sojourn with the queen. Some even oscillate between the two. So, for example, it is debated whether his adventures with Jason and the other Argonauts occurred during his time with Eurystheus or Omphale. This voyage is notable for many things, but one of the more interesting is the way in which Hercules' activities lead him to be written into the history of homosexuality. On this voyage, we find Hercules enamoured of Hylas, the beautiful youth for whom he has developed a passion. So strong is Hercules' desire for the young man that he abandons Jason and his crew to look for Hylas when he goes missing after being abducted and ravished by nymphs.

The second-century Christian writer Clement of Alexandria saw the relationship between Hercules and Hylas as just another sign of pagan immorality. However, Hercules' desire ensured that the name of Hylas was on the lips of almost every nineteenth-century homosexual aesthete and apologist. Numerous poems and essays recall his astonishing good looks. His story with its associations of youth, beauty, sex and death (the nymphs in their passions drag him to a watery doom) appealed to the sensibilities of the *fin-de-siècle*. In 1896, critics heaped praise on John William Waterhouse's painting of the fatal meeting between Hylas and the Nymphs. Indeed, Hylas achieves a popularity which is not matched by his more famous lover. Hercules is largely absent from the nineteenth century. Romanticism is partly to blame. Hercules was perceived as lacking human flaws and the introspection they generated. He was too robust to be a true Romantic hero.

One of the most popular stories attributed to his time with Omphale recalls his capture of the two robbers called the Cercopes (the 'monkey men'). They were brothers whose extensive criminal activities made them a by-word for illegal behaviour. According to one tradition, their mother prophesied that they would meet their doom at the hands of the 'black bottom'. This they interpreted as meaning some-body black-skinned. They realised their error when they foolishly tried to steal Hercules' weapons. When he caught them, he tied their feet to a pole, slung it over his shoulders and carried them dangling upside down back to town. In this position, they were brought to the realisation of the correctness of their mother's prophecy. Directly in front of their eyes were Hercules' sun-blackened buttocks. The scene of Hercules carrying the captured thieves over his shoulders occurs in a number of vase-paintings and temple sculptures from the sixth century BC onwards. One of the best and ear-liest examples is found on a metope from Temple 'C' in Selinus. Here we see the two thieves hanging on either side of the hero, their archaic curls flapping in the breeze.

Hercules eventually released this criminal pair either because he was so amused by the jokes they told each other as they hung upside down or because of the entreaties of their mother. Such clemency is unusual in the hero. More typical is his treatment of the villainous Syleus, who forced passers-by to work in his vineyard and then rewarded their efforts by murdering them with a hoe. Hercules slaughters him without compunction; he also rips up the vineyard and kills Syleus' daughter for good measure.

Death and Apotheosis

Hercules' period of service with Omphale marks an interlude in a narrative arc that leads from his triumph in his labours to his death on Mount Oeta. The ancient biographies of Hercules promote this sense of imminent destruction by portraying the period after his service with Omphale as one in which the hero settles scores and ties up loose ends.

As he promised, Hercules returned to Troy to avenge himself on King Laomedon on account of the latter's refusal to pay Hercules for rescuing his daughter. Hercules' Trojan War has clear parallels with its Homeric counterpart. Hercules arrives with a fleet of ships manned by volunteers from various parts of the Greek world. His opponents initially manage to beat back his forces to their ships. After a long siege, he eventually breaches the walls and sacks the city, murdering the king and his sons. Like Odysseus, he suffers storms and shipwrecks as he attempts to return home.

His adventures in Troy are notable for two events. The first occurs when the walls of the city are finally breached. Hercules entered Troy only to find that one of his companions, Telamon, had managed to beat him to the honour of entering first. Enraged, Hercules picked up his sword and charged at Telamon. Luckily the brave youth was saved by some quick thinking. Seeing the fury of the hero, he bent down to pick up some stones. When Hercules questioned him about his actions, he replied that the hero had caught him in the act of building an altar to Hercules the Victor. We find an almost identical story is told about Alexander the Great. Such tales both remind one about the prerogatives of status that apply during war and, at the same time, under-cut the pompousness of commanders who insist on their observance.

The second significant incident occurs when Hercules decides to reward Telamon by presenting him with Hesione, the daughter of Laomedon, as booty. To accompany her on her journey, Hesione was allowed to choose any captive. She chose her only surviving brother, Podarces. However, before Hercules would allow him to accompany her, he demanded that Hesione ransom her brother. This she does by removing her veil and handing it over to the hero. Her beauty buys the young prince, and, at the same time, gives him a new name – Priam (from the Greek *priamai* 'to buy').

Hercules wreaks a similar campaign of revenge against King Augeas who refused to pay him for clearing out the stables. Again, Hercules invades the country at the head of an army. Augeas and his allies led by the Siamese-twin generals Eurytus and Cteatus are defeated and Hercules establishes one of his allies, Augeas' son Phyleus on the throne. Nothing seems to be able to stop Hercules as he avenges himself for every minor slight that he or his friends have suffered. Not even the gods can restrain him. In the course of his campaigns, Hera gets an arrow in her breast, Hercules slashes Ares' thigh, and wounds Hades. It is only when he decides to revenge himself on the kingdom of Oechalia for their refusal to grant him the hand of Iole in marriage that this brutal momentum is halted – stopped dead in its tracks.

By this time, Hercules was already involved with a woman called Deianeira. Her name says it all. In Greek, it means 'man killer' or 'husband killer'. Needless to say, it does not seem to have been a popular choice for daughters in antiquity. She was the daughter of Oeneus, the King of the Caledonians, and the sister of the hero Meleager. According to some accounts, the spirit of Meleager begged Hercules to marry his sister when Hercules visited the Underworld to retrieve Cerberus. To gain her as his wife, Hercules first needed to wrestle with the river god Achelous. This god is commonly portrayed as possessing a human face attached to the front half of a bull which is then joined to a scaly, finned serpent's tail. Deianeira's reluctance for this suitor is understandable. In the course of their wrestling bout, Hercules breaks off one of Achelous' horns. In order to retrieve it, Achelous offers in exchange the Horn of Amalthea, the cornucopia that supplies abundant meat and drink of whatever type one desires.

Hercules' courtship of Deianeira is beset by problems. As has happened so many times before, Hercules' anger leads him accidentally to kill one of the royal pages and the couple are forced to go into exile. As they make their journey from the land of the Caledonians, they come to the river Evenus. Here the centaur Nessus offers to ferry the couple across the river one at a time. Oddly, Hercules' experience with lustful centaurs fails to warn him that this is just a ruse so that Nessus can spirit Deianeira away for himself. Nessus' plan nearly works. He manages to make it almost entirely across the river before Hercules' arrows put a speedy end to his designs. As he dies, Nessus professes his love to Deianeira and tells her that should she ever need a love potion to ensure that Hercules' affections do not stray then she should gather up the blood from around his wound and administer it to the hero.

Nessus' words prove prophetic. A year or so later, having destroyed the kingdom of Oechalia, Hercules finds that there is no longer any impediment to his union with Iole. Fearing that she is about to be displaced by this younger and more beautiful rival, Deianeira smears Nessus' blood on the fine clothes that Hercules has requested so that he can make a sacrifice to Zeus in thanksgiving for his victory over the Oechalians. These garments are carried to Hercules by the page Lichas. The moment Hercules dons the garments, the hydra's poison which lurked within Nessus' blood begins to take effect. The clothes cling and burn Hercules' flesh with a fire that cannot be extinguished. In his agony, he picks up Lichas and hurls him into the sea where he is transformed into a man-shaped rock used by Greek sailors for navigation purposes in the classical period. Finding the pain unbearable, Hercules mounts a pyre that he has built on the side of Mount Oeta. As the flames rise, the spirit of Hercules leaves the mortal realm.

Even to this day, the heat generated by the hydra's garments is purported to warm a mountain spring, which gives this place its name – Thermopylae (Gk. 'gates of fire'). It was here that one of Hercules' supposed descendants, the Spartan King Leonidas, would also die in his attempt to hold back the Persian army as they invaded Greece. Ludicrously out-numbered, he never really stood a chance. David links the tragedy of Leonidas' death with that of his illustrious ancestor in his famous portrait of the king. Behind Leonidas, ominously in the background, is an altar to the hero. Indeed, in preliminary sketches for the painting, David even had the spirit of Hercules standing behind the king, rousing the Spartans to battle.

David's use of the death of Hercules as a tragic marker continues a tradition which extends back into antiquity. The most influential version of this story is the tragedy by the Athenian playwright Sophocles. Unfortunately, we do not know when precisely his version was staged. Sophocles' career spans most of the fifth century BC and it is not clear whether this is an early or a late play.

The drama opens with Deianeira worried that she has been abandoned by Hercules from whom she has heard nothing in over a year. Her anxieties are compounded when she hears that Hercules is waging war against Oechalia. It has been prophesied that this campaign will bring either an end to Hercules' toil or his death. She sends one of her sons by Hercules to give him aid.

At this point, Lichas arrives announcing the victory and the imminent return of Hercules. Lichas brings with him a train of captives including Iole. However, Deianeira's delight is quickly soured as another messenger reports the real story of the campaign. Lust was its driving force. Hercules' love for Iole led him to wage this terrible war and now he intends to throw over Deianeira for Iole.

After wringing confirmation of this state of affairs from Lichas, Deianeira retrieves the vial of Nessus' blood that she has kept to apply to Hercules' clothes. Nessus had warned her that in order for this blood to work its magic it must never be exposed to light or flame until the moment of its use. As a result, Deianeira applies the blood in darkness and sends Hercules' clothes in a locked box.

Deianeira soon learns of the terrible consequences of her actions when on the following day she notices a ray of sunlight hit a scrap of wool that she used to dab the blood on to the clothes. Instantly, it bursts into violent flame and produces a dark poisonous foam. Her fears about her actions are confirmed when her son returns telling of the agony which Hercules now finds himself in. Traumatised by her actions, Deianeira retires into the house. Moments later a nurse appears to recount how Deianeira has committed violent suicide.

At this point, Hercules enters on to the stage swearing vengeance on his wife. His son breaks the news to him that he has arrived too late and explains that Deianeira was only acting from desperate, pitiable motives. As Hercules begins to comprehend the sequence of events, he starts to rail against the gods and the unfair lot of men. Suicide is the only option and he lays the most difficult charge a father can upon his son and asks him to prepare the funeral pyre so that he can die. Reluctantly, the son acquiesces.

The impact of Sophocles' play can be traced in a number of works. We know that it impressed Cicero, who produced a translation of one of its main speeches. There was a Latin version which has been attributed to Seneca. One of the more unusual retellings of the story comes in a poem from Ovid's *Heroides*. These poems are written in the form of fictional letters from famous women of mythology to their lovers. Among the correspondence, we find a suicide note from Deianeira to Hercules. She berates him for his treatment of her. Abandoned, she is left only with her fears for his safety. Her sleep is disturbed by nightmares about wild boars, lions, three-headed hounds and hissing snakes. In the course of her criticism, she exposes the contradictions in his personality. She finds it impossible to reconcile the hero who makes the world safe and can bear the heavens on his shoulders with the weakling who can be overcome by the first pretty face that comes along. Deianeira is right. Hercules is an enigma. From the abundance of tales about him, it is impossible to create a truly rounded character with internal consistency. She explodes the biographical project. Even at the point of his death, we don't really know who he is. He seems to be just a collection of marvellous stories. Hercules barely stays still long enough for us to comprehend him fully.

Part of the reason for the success of Sophocles' play lies in its ability to speak to contemporary concerns. One of the constant themes of tragedy is male fear of female plotting. The Greek perception of the domestic realm as a female space meant that men were concerned about women's ability to cause them harm through control of it. Concomitant with this fear is a fear of female poison and magic. Indeed, poison and magic were flip sides of the same coin. Love magic was often conceived as a type of poison which saps the victim's strength and control until they are unable to resist the unwanted advances of their lover. It would be easy to dismiss such fears as ludicrous, just the typical product of a misogynist outlook which sought to ensure that privileged public space remained a male preserve and felt guilty about sidelining women and relegating them to indoors. However, before we do so, we might like to consider a real murder case from fifth-century BC Athens.

The case was brought by a young man against his stepmother for the murder of his father. He alleged that his stepmother hatched a plot against her husband and used as her agent the courtesan of a mutual friend and neighbour. This woman was desperate because she thought she was about to be abandoned by her lover. The stepmother, knowing that her husband and the courtesan's lover would be sacrificing together, allegedly tricked the courtesan by giving her poison which she claimed was a love potion that could be administered in the wine they would use to pour their libations. Horrified the courtesan watched her lover and his guest die as they drank from the poisoned cup. This transposition of the Deianeira story into a domestic setting raises a number of questions about the relationship between myth and real life. Are the fears that myth expresses all too real? If you repeat a story enough times, will people absorb it to the extent that they start to act it out? Or has a disaffected son managed to hijack a mythological narrative to give some plausibility to an otherwise fanciful case? The case of the poisoning stepmother puts front and centre debates about the nature of myth. If we believe the prosecution and convict her, we commit ourselves to a strong version of myth's truth-telling abilities. If we see through the artifice of this account, we are forced to accept that myth's claims are weaker. Are we prepared to take this risk? The prosecution hopes not.

Sophocles' play ends with a procession towards the funeral pyre. It leaves the fate of Hercules ambiguous. Usually, heroes join other mortals as shadows in the realm of Hades. Their earthly bodies still contain some force. Their bones are magical and their graves require regular sacrifice. At crucial moments, they can even reappear to offer assistance to the living. Certainly, there is an early tradition in which this is the fate of Hercules. A fragment of a very early work called the *Catalogue of Women* preserves a version in which Deianeira's actions lead to Hercules' shade joining those who dwell in the Underworld. However, there is a competing tradition which has Hercules, his mortal form burnt away, joining the immortal gods on Olympus. Here he is finally reconciled with Hera who performs a ritual adopting him as a son. To complete the joyful picture, he marries the goddess Hebe. This tradition of apotheosis would also seem to be quite old. We have a number of early vases in which Hercules can be seen arriving on a chariot at Olympus guided by his patroness Athena.

The gaps between these two stories allow Hercules to have a number of identities. He is both hero and god, and was worshipped as such. In crashing through the barrier that separates mortal and divine, Hercules created a new area of theological speculation and injected a note of ambivalence in his relationship with the early Christian church. On the one hand, Hercules' popularity posed a threat to the new religion. We have already seen that writers such as Clement of

Alexandria were only too happy to denounce him. At the same time, he provided perhaps one of the best ways to make the gospel story explicable. He seems ready-made for a narrative about the son of God who dies suffering and becomes divine. In early Christian art, we find biblical stories being juxtaposed with stories from the Hercules cycle. Even his journey for the apples of Hesperides was seen as a proto-Eden adventure: Hercules wiping out the snake that guarded the apples rather than succumbing like Eve to its seductive charms.

Hercules' apotheosis became a standard Christian allegory for the resurrection from the period of the Renaissance onwards. Rubens painted Hercules assisting Henri IV into heaven while his widow mourned his passing in the world below. Lemoyne decorated the *Grand Appartement* of Versailles with a spectacular painted ceiling on the subject. It stunned the court, and Louis XV made him Chief Painter to the King as a result. The painting is a remarkable achievement. With an area of over 480 square metres it is one of the largest paintings ever executed. In luminous colour, Lemoyne presents us with one hundred and forty-two different figures. Yet, there is only one who really grabs our attention. Through the painting's dizzying use of perspective, we feel the precariousness of Hercules' position. Lemoyne knew all about the fragility of the spirit. Six months after he completed this canvas, he committed suicide. One slip and Hercules could topple to the floor to join us. Lesser characters already seem to be falling by the wayside. As with all of us, Hercules' place in heaven is not guaranteed. It requires intercession. We see a case being made. This pagan soul has become truly Christianised.

Indeed, the early Christians were heirs to a large philosophical tradition about the procedure by which one became a god. The fifth-century BC philosopher Empedocles purportedly tried to convince people that he had become a god by causing his body to vaporise as he leapt into the crater of a volcano. Doubts were raised only once people noticed one of his bronze sandals floating in the lava. Others claimed that people were all gods or would be reborn as such. For the Romans, such issues became more pertinent once the deification of the emperors became a more regular event. The Roman writer Lucian satirises all this speculation about the process of becoming divine in one of his *Dialogues of the Dead*, fictional dialogues between famous characters set in the Underworld. In one he has the shade of Hercules meet the cynic philosopher Diogenes. Diogenes expresses surprise at seeing the spirit in the Underworld. The shade explains that he is not the real Hercules, merely his 'form'. As half-man, half-god, Hercules has been split between Olympus and the Underworld. However, Diogenes is not prepared to accept this explanation and quizzes the spirit further. How can 'form' be split? Even if this was possible, how do we know that it is not the real Hercules down in the Underworld and the 'form' that is enjoying the pleasures of Heaven? In any case, when did this splitting occur? At the point of conception? Were there always two Herculeses? Or did it occur at the moment of death? Diogenes even goes so far as to suggest that there might be three heroes – one that was burnt on Mount Oeta in addition to the other two. Such philosophic speculation proves all too much for Hercules who gives up in disgust. Diogenes mocks those who get caught up in the details of Hercules' life. Sometimes it is better to go with the flow and accept the marvellous.

The Afterlife

What sort of world does Hercules leave in his wake? One
of the topics much discussed in antiquity is the fate of his
children. Like everything else about him, Hercules' sex-
drive was prodigious. The most complete list of his offspring
records sixty-seven sons by sixty different women (with the
typical chauvinism of the ancient Greeks, nobody seemed
interested in cataloguing daughters). Yet even this list con-
tains gaps. Other authors give estimates of over one hundred
children. It is doubtful if Hercules, had he been quizzed,
would have known the number. As myth's 'love rat', his
approach to fatherhood is exemplified by his complete surprise at discovering Telephus, the son he produced after a
one-night stand with the priestess Auge. As a priestess of
Athena, Auge was supposed to remain chaste and so the

child was exposed on a mountainside. Here it was raised by a doe who had recently lost her faun. Hercules' accidental discovery of his son while on his wanderings was popular in Hellenistic art, which particularly loved the juxtaposition of the tiny, soft child with the hard, mature adult male. The scene appears in a Roman wall-painting from the so-called 'Basilica' at Herculaneum, a painting which subsequently influenced work by Ingres and Picasso. It also features in a frieze from the interior of the Great Altar to Zeus at Pergamum depicting a complete narrative of the life of Telephus, the mythical founder of Pergamum. Yet, for all the pleasure that Hercules seems to express at the discovery of his son, what the episodic nature of this frieze makes clear is just how small a part he played in Telephus' life. Hercules is only there for a couple of scenes and then he disappears from the picture. Hercules comes across as a bit of a 'dead-beat dad'. In a world which prized the father–son relationship above all else, Hercules is a failure.

Forced to fend for themselves, the children of Hercules were pursued by his enemies, most notably Eurystheus. The story of Eurystheus' persecution of the children was a popular one in Athens. The assistance that Athens gave to the children on this occasion was remembered in speeches given at the funerals of the war dead, and on the tragic stage. After much wandering, these children eventually settled in the Peloponnese and subsequently founded all the principal aristocratic houses of the region. In ancient Greece, every member of the Peloponnesian elite from the kings of Sparta downwards claimed descent from Hercules, and justified their superior status on this basis.

Mythographers traditionally finish their stories about the exploits of Hercules with his children. In focusing on his descendants, they attempt to build a bridge between their own period and the mythical past. In this sense, the 'children of Hercules' are partly allegorical. Their lines of descent create a connection that explains and validates contemporary regimes and mores. We might attempt something similar. In trying to express Hercules' impact on the twentieth and twenty-first centuries, we will find that 'the children of Hercules' still live and walk among us. They have merely left the rugged Peloponnese for the more hospitable climes of Malibu and Venice Beach.

In many ways, it is appropriate that a story that began on the Bay of Naples should end on the beaches of Los Angeles. Both are places which mix industry with pleasure and where pleasure is an industry. Although in all his wanderings Hercules never got this far west, we can see his legacy in the rippling abdominals of California's health-conscious citizenry and most especially in its favourite son, Arnold Schwarzenegger. The process that formed the current Governor of California's extraordinary body (famously described as 'a brown condom stuffed with walnuts') is one whose origins lie at the end of the nineteenth century. In the last few decades of this century, ideas about health and public hygiene intersected with classical aesthetics and vaudeville showmanship to produce a new kind of body – that of 'the modern Hercules'.

Hercules

Conventionally the modern art of bodybuilding was born on 12 June 1893. That evening the audience of the Casino Roof-Garden on Broadway in New York witnessed a performance of bodily display quite unlike anything else they had seen before. The evening had begun convention-ally enough. The first act had featured a popular musical burlesque entitled *Adonis* in which, in a reversal of the Pygmalion myth, a female sculptress brought a male statue (the Adonis of the title) to life. The farce ended with the statue, having been pursued by a gaggle of lusty, grotesque women, leaping back on to his pedestal and begging the gods to restore him to his previous marmoreal state. As the actor froze and the curtain descended the audience could see that this request had been granted. What the audience were not expecting was that the curtain would rise almost immediately to reveal a different figure on the pedestal. In place of Adonis, their eyes feasted on 'the most perfectly developed body in the world'. Eugene Sandow, the father of modern bodybuilding, had arrived. To the increasing astonishment of the audience, Sandow slowly struck a number of poses designed to show his highly developed musculature. According to a contemporary reviewer, 'It was hard for the spectators . . . to believe that it was indeed flesh and blood that they beheld. Such knots and bunches and layers of muscles they had never seen before off the statue of an Achilles, a Discobolus, or a fighting gladiator.' There had never been a living body quite like this one. While the comparisons offered here by the reviewer were in terms of Achilles and gladiators, the word most

commonly used to describe the look that Sandow pio-
neered was 'Herculean'.

There had, of course, been numerous strongmen
throughout the nineteenth century who had cast themselves
as the 'new Hercules'. The standard uniform of the circus
strongman was the lion/leopard skin draped in imitation of
Hercules, and carnival imagery was replete with classical
allusions designed to add touches of exoticism and class to
the various acts. So, for example, a trip to the circus could
involve such performances as *The Flying Mercury*, *Alexander
the Great and Thalestris the Amazon*, the Ringling brothers'
Cleopatra, and the *Last Days of Pompeii*. The most elaborate of
these classically inspired shows was Barnum and Bailey's
Nero, or the Destruction of Rome. Staged in Olympia in
London in 1888, this performance boasted a cast of 2,000
performers, 100 massive golden chariots, wild beasts, and
combined 'gladiatorial contests of the famed Coliseum and
Circus Maximus with the Olympic Games of ancient
Greece'.

What distinguished Sandow from his predecessors was
the nature of his physique. Size rather than muscular definition was the distinctive feature of the traditional circus
strongman. Bulk was achieved without reference to form.
Illustrations and photographs reveal barrel-chested giants
with bodies that, more often than not, ran to fat rather than
muscle. Indeed, as a large number of strongman tricks were
nothing more than stage illusions, these performers had little
need for actual physical strength.

In contrast, Sandow's background lay in the celebrity

Hercules

weights movement which had swept Germany and then quickly spread throughout the rest of Europe. Born Friedrich Wilhelm Müller, he became the associate of Professor Louis Attila, a man who claimed to have taught exercise to Tsar Alexander III, King George of Greece and Edward VII of England. Sandow first came to prominence as a result of winning a strength competition at the Royal Aquarium judged by, among others, the Marquess of Queensberry. Appropriately, for someone with the physique of Hercules, his opponent in the competition rejoiced in the stage name of 'Cyclops'.

Sandow made clear his debt to the classical past throughout his act and publicity. In his largely fictional autobiography, Sandow claims that it was the inspiration of classical statuary that provided the impetus for him to transform himself from an 'exceedingly delicate' child to a modern colossus. Certainly, the poses that he adopted in his act were all derived from classical sculpture. These poses in imitation of statuary would eventually form the basis of the first ever bodybuilding competition held in the Royal Albert Hall in September 1901. Among the judges on this occasion was Sir Arthur Conan Doyle. They also lie behind a number of the poses used in modern bodybuilding competitions. Prominent among the poses Sandow adopted was his imitation of the Farnese Hercules. Photographs show Sandow imitated the statue right down to the inclusion of props such as a club draped with animal skin. The only significant deviation is a large fig leaf designed to cover his genitals, although even this mimicked contemporary practice for the display of Greek statuary.

It is hard to overstate the influence of the Farnese Hercules on the popular conceptions of the 'Hercules' look. It was widely copied almost from the moment of its excavation from the Baths of Caracalla. Casts of the statue found their way into most major museums and art schools. Look at almost any painting showing collections of classical statues or antiquities and you will find it lurking somewhere in the background. In coming to represent the canonical image of Hercules, the statue erases a number of other competing images from antiquity. Not every image of Hercules portrayed him as such a muscle-bound hunk. The Etruscans, for example, often preferred to depict their version of Hercules as slim-hipped, almost feminine. Few gave him muscles quite as overdeveloped as those of the Farnese Hercules. Hercules had to be built for speed and agility, not just strength; after all, one of his labours had been to chase a swift-footed hind for over a year. It is hard to imagine the Farnese Hercules with its massive bulk ever reaching any great speed or its tremendous thighs allowing much long-distance running.

However, as Sandow soon found to his cost, it occasionally requires more than the right look to pass as the modern Hercules. Perhaps his most spectacular failure occurred in San Francisco in May 1894 when he decided to reprise Hercules' first labour and single-handedly wrestle with a lion. Unfortunately, the audience which turned up to watch the spectacle was treated to a less than heroic performance. Sandow ensured that the lion was muzzled and its claws covered by leather mittens before he even entered the ring. In addition, he chose a lion who, either through age or because it was drugged, refused to put up any fight. In desperation, Sandow was reduced to pulling its tail in an attempt to get some reaction. The crowd booed and hissed. Shouts of 'fake' mixed with derisive laughter. The performance was a flop and Sandow never fought a lion again.

This incident with the lion represents an unusual blemish in an otherwise faultless campaign of self-promotion. Assisted by Florenz Ziegfeld of the Trocadero theatre in Chicago, Sandow ensured that he dominated the popular media. Photographs of him circulated widely, especially among an admiring female audience. Newspapers carried numerous articles about his amazing feats. He gave lectures to the students of Harvard and groups of army cadets. The army cadets were even invited to run their hands over his torso, a sensation described as like running your hands 'over corrugated iron'. The phrase 'washboard stomach' was coined to describe his abdominals. On the strength of his fame, Sandow was able to publish some of the first ever physical fitness magazines, and his image was used to promote equipment such as 'Sandow's Combined Developer'. The British Museum even commissioned a nude plaster cast of Sandow to exhibit as the 'ideal European man'.

In many ways the Sandow phenomenon typifies passions at the turn of the century. This was a period in which all sorts of new causes were taken up with equal, seemingly indiscriminate, enthusiasm. Some such as 'women's education' and 'female suffrage' were destined to last. Others such as 'thorough mastication', the health craze promoted by Horace Fletcher for chewing food until it liquefied (roughly a hundred chews per mouthful), proved to be more short-lived affairs. All the initial signs were that Sandow and his culture of physical development might well pass as just another fad. It did not take long before people began to feel that there was something unhealthy in spending so much time gazing at these near-naked bodies that did not seem to do anything. By measuring arms and chests in centimetres rather than by their ability to work or play sport, these bodies appeared decadent and narcissistic.

The rise of 'beefcake' photography – the name is a humorous play on the sexualised images of women known as 'cheesecake' shots – merely cemented its unwholesome reputation. Designed for a largely gay audience, these photographs combined many of the poses and props from the field of bodybuilding with the erotic tradition of the *tableau vivant*. The sport of bodybuilding has long denied that there is anything erotic about its displays, and one of the earliest regulations passed by the International Federation of Bodybuilders (IFBB) was the prohibition on competitors appearing in nude photographs or shots showing any genitalia. However, despite such denials, it was often hard to tell where pornography ended and physical display began. As early as 1910, the magazine *Physical Culture* found itself prosecuted for the transmission of obscene material through the mail service.

Despite successes such as Charles Atlas' famous series of 'I can make you a man' advertisements, the world of bodybuilding seemed destined to become an obscure subculture, suitable only for risqué stage-shows such as the 'Mae West

Review'. What it needed was a wholesome hero. The choice it settled on was Hercules. However, it took Steve Reeves' amazing physique, an unprecedented studio publicity campaign, and some of the most cringe-worthy dubbing ever seen to reawaken Hercules' popular appeal and provide the flabby, disempowered, office-bound men of post-war America with a figure they could aspire to be.

The extraordinary success of Steve Reeves' *Hercules* (1957, original title *Le fatiche di Ercole*) was unprecedented. Smashing all previous records, it was seen by 24 million people and made up to $18 million at the box-office on its American release in 1959, catapulting its star to fame and fortune. Although the winner of Mr America (1947), Mr World (1948) and Mr Universe (1950), Reeves was little known outside the field of bodybuilding before this film. It almost single-handedly revitalised the Italian film industry. Film finance began to pour in from foreign sources, allowing the industry to change from a collection of parochial studios focused on producing material for domestic consumption into important international players. The key figure behind this success was the film's promoter Joseph E. Levine. His publicity campaign overturned all the conventions of contemporary movie promotion. Having acquired the film rights for $120,000, he then arranged a publicity campaign whose cost has been estimated at close to $1 million. At its launch party at the Waldorf-Astoria in New York, Levine described his style of publicity as 'Hercules explodation' because 'we are going to explode Hercules throughout the nation this summer'. It was no idle boast. Levine took out full-page advertisements in over 130 magazines. Giant bill-board posters of Hercules appeared in almost every town in America. A two-storey-high cutout of Reeves as Hercules

Joseph E. Levine and Steve Reeves on the set of *Hercules Unchained*, 1959.

toured the country. Levine also block-booked hundreds of theatres to show the film, pioneering the modern procedure of saturation booking on a movie's release.

More importantly, this film inspired countless imitations. Almost immediately Reeves was commissioned to star in a sequel, *Hercules Unchained* (1959, original title *Ercole e la Regina di Lidia*), which was the subject of a similarly lavish publicity campaign. Its launch party, for example, featured a colossal ice-carving of Hercules, his muscles illuminated by light bulbs of different colours.

Many other Italian film production companies were keen to profit from the Hercules franchise. The Italian film industry had an already established tradition of low-budget melodramas set in antiquity. Traditionally Roman themes had been most popular. Early examples include *Gli Ultimi Giorni di Pompei* (1908, 'The Last Days of Pompeii') and *Quo Vadis?* (1913). Many of these movies featured a local strongman called Maciste who made his first appearance beating up Carthaginians in the film *Cabiria* (1914). Yet it was the success of *Hercules* which revitalised this tradition and kicked production into overdrive. In the decade following *Hercules'* release over 170 films set in antiquity were produced, more than sixty featuring the name 'Hercules' in their US or UK titles. These movies were called 'pepla' by French film critics on account of the extremely short tunics worn by their male leads – a name that has stuck. So prevalent was this genre that it even inspired parodies such as *The Three Stooges Meet Hercules*.

This demand for films meant a corresponding demand for bodies. In the early 1960s there was a veritable conveyor belt from the gyms of California and New York to the film sets of southern Italy. Ironically, these English-speaking actors would then find themselves re-dubbed into English for US and UK release. The list of actors who have played Hercules reads like a roll call of the most illustrious names in bodybuilding. Mark Forest (Mr Venice Beach, 1954), Reg Park (Mr Universe, 1951, 1958 and 1965), Peter Lupus (Mr International Health Physique, 1960), Reg Lewis (Mr Universe, 1957) and Mickey Hargitay (Mr Universe, 1955) all lined up for the role. Perhaps the most famous body-builder to play Hercules was Arnold Schwarzenegger (Mr Europe, 1966; Mr Universe 1967–70; Mr World, 1970; Mr Olympia, 1970–75 and 1980), who was the star of the flop *Hercules in New York* (1970, aka 'Hercules Goes Bananas'). Though the film was produced in America, Schwarzen-egger's strong Austrian accent meant that the tradition of dubbing-in the lead actor's voice had to be continued. It was particularly fitting that Schwarzenegger should end up play-ing Hercules. According to his bodybuilding memoir, it was seeing peplum classics such as *Hercules, Hercules Unchained* and *Hercules and the Captive Women* that inspired him to take up bodybuilding. Indeed, *Hercules and the Captive Women* featured Reg Park, Schwarzenegger's eventual bodybuilding coach, in the title role.

While all these films had a very strong commitment to a distinctive 'Herculean' look, their makers felt absolutely no loyalty to the mythic tradition surrounding Hercules, and freely altered and invented storylines for the hero. Despite the promises made in the Italian title of *Hercules* that this film concerned the labours (*le fatiche*) of Hercules, only two of them managed to make an appearance in the movie, the subjugation of the Nemean lion and the Cretan bull. Instead, the film is largely a reworking of the story of Jason and the Argonauts. Apollonius of Rhodes, the author of an epic on the topic, is even awarded a script credit in the opening

Hercules and the Captive Women. Film poster, 1961.

titles. A similar approach was adopted with its sequel, *Hercules Unchained*. This time Aeschylus' *Seven Against Thebes* was used as the basis for the plot, with Hercules inserted into this story about the feud between the children of Oedipus over who should succeed to his throne. Yet even antiquity soon could not provide enough thrilling storylines to fill demand. So we see Hercules going out to fight even more exotic and outlandish opponents such as the sons of Kubla Khan (*Hercules against the Mongols*, 1964), vampires (*Hercules and the Haunted World*, 1961), Aztecs (*Hercules against the Sons of the Sun*, 1966), bug-eyed aliens (*Hercules against the Moon Men*, 1964), and the radioactive army of the deranged Queen of Atlantis (*Hercules and the Captive Women*, 1961).

Thrills and titillation were what these Hercules films promised and delivered. It is no coincidence that in the original *Hercules* Steve Reeves and his crew found themselves washed up on the island home of a pack of sex-starved Amazons. Nor that the audience learns of these women's sinister intent only after they have been forced to endure scenes of Amazons frolicking on the beach in wet, nipple-hugging tunics and revealing their thighs in an evening dance spectacular. These erotic dance sequences became a mainstay of the genre. The poster for *Hercules and the Captive Women* prominently asks, 'What weird sadistic ritual was the secret of these women?' The audience was probably not surprised to discover that it involved skimpy costuming, thrusting pelvises and an oriental drum beat.

It is appropriate that one of the first marketing tie-ins for Steve Reeves' *Hercules* was a series of Dell comic books; the strip cartoon is where this version of Hercules belongs. Both the popular TV series *Hercules: The Legendary Journeys*, starring Kevin Sorbo, and Disney's animated *Hercules* are its direct descendants. What unifies these works with the peplum tradition is that they are not terribly interested in engaging with the underlying mentalities that produced the Hercules cycle of stories. Their heroes are the generic heroes of the comic book. Ron Clement, the director of Disney's *Hercules*, admits as much: 'Hercules appealed to us partly because it didn't seem as sacred a thing as something like the *Odyssey*. We had to feel that whatever we chose, we would be able to take quite a few liberties . . . We were thinking of a kind of superhero – the first superhero.' Quite a few liberties is an understatement. Disney's Hercules is an awkward adolescent whose greatest desire is to find out 'where he belongs' (a sentiment belted out in appropriately cheesy lyrics by Michael Bolton). His is a character-type that Disney had already perfected in *Aladdin* and the *Lion King*. In keeping with conservative family values, the film makes Hercules not the product of an adulterous fling, but a child abduction victim who was whisked away from his loving parents Hera and Zeus while they slept on Mt Olympus (the realm of the gods is imagined as an exclusive gated-community). In a move that stretches the limits of postmodern irony, Disney names his love interest Meg after the wife traditionally murdered by Hercules in a maddened rampage. At the end of the film, when offered immortality and a place on Olympus, Hercules rejects the offer. He has found out that the place where he belongs is right there on earth in Megara's arms. The audience is left to gag into their popcorn.

Given the rich tradition of representations that we have already explored, it is easy to dismiss this reduction of

Hercules to the level of just another superhero. Megara in Disney's *Hercules* begins her main love song with the line 'If there's a prize for rotten judgement, I guess I've won that.' Certainly, there has been no end of educated readers who have lined up to agree. Yet, in doing so, we should be careful not to miss what is important about this cultural moment. Even in antiquity people realised that the monuments we make to Hercules might be unrecognisable to some. Certainly that seems to be the message found on a southern Italian column crater in the collection of the Metropolitan Museum of Art, New York. Here we see a young unbearded Hercules coming upon an artist who is putting the finishing touches to a statue of the hero. Hercules looks on in puzzled amazement. He clearly does not know what to make of the scene that confronts him. This image is probably an allusion to a story about the inventor Daedalus who built a statue to Hercules to thank him for finding the body of Daedalus' son, Icarus, and giving it a proper burial. Hercules comes across the statue one evening and, mistaking it in the dull light for an opponent, proceeds to take it on in a fight. While it is easy to see dim but pugnacious Hercules as the butt of the joke here, we should not let Daedalus get away unscathed. Certainly what seems to have intrigued the artist of the vase-painting is the notion of misrecognition implicit in the story. How could Hercules not recognise a statue of himself? What is the point of creating a monument out of gratitude, if the intended recipient doesn't even pick up the message of thanks? Or are such monuments really only ever about making us feel good about ourselves?

Hercules

No one can deny the entertainment value of the cinematic versions of Hercules, even if one chooses to enjoy them only as examples of high camp. Indeed, one could easily mount an argument that peplum films represent the largest and most popular classicising movement in the past two hundred years, a Drive-in Renaissance. Their success was replicated by the Disney *Hercules* which made a $245 million profit, and the extraordinary viewing figures for the *Legendary Journeys*. Such works challenge any notion that the classical world is only the preserve of intellectual elites or that the Hercules name has lost any of its appeal. One cannot doubt these films' sincerity. The ancient Greece that they created may not have been accurate, but intriguingly their world was always recognisable as Greece. These films remind us that Greece possesses a number of potent symbols in its imagery. A whitened column, a short tunic, a key meander painted on a wall are all it takes to transport us there. Unsurprisingly, it is this visual language that the Disney executives, marketeers and brand professionals *par excellence*, understand best. Where Disney's *Hercules* succeeds is not in its storyline, but in its look. The film cleverly plays on the huge reservoir of classical imagery that forms part of the Western cultural heritage. Roman sarcophagi, the full repertoire of red- and black-figure vase-painting, the temple of Zeus at Olympia, Minoan frescoes all make an appearance in this movie. They are its real stars. Even the drops of water fall in the shape of Greek vases. Greece need not only be substance, it can also be surface. Fail to understand this and you fail to appreciate how Greece really works.

It remains to be seen what the twenty-first century will make of Hercules. As the wide variety of Herculeses I have presented demonstrates, it is clear that he can be taken in many directions. Charlton Heston's voice-over at the start of Disney's *Hercules* asks 'But what makes a true hero?' While it is true that no one from antiquity (or indeed no one apart from a North American adolescent) would have understood the answer that Disney provided, we may nevertheless concur that it is a question worth posing. The answer lies with us. It was the sixth-century BC philosopher Xenophanes of Colophon who first argued that we create gods in our own image. The same applies, only more so, for our heroes.

Le Fin

4/8/09

Notes and Bibliography

General Works

ANCIENT SOURCES

The most complete accounts of Hercules' life and exploits are found in:

The Library of Apollodorus 2.4.5–2.7.8. A summary of myths written in the first or second centuries AD and attributed to Apollodorus, one of the last great Alexandrian intellectuals.

Diodorus Siculus 4.8-39. Diodorus was a first-century BC writer who wrote a universal history from mythological times to his own day.

Hercules

INTRODUCTIONS TO THE HERCULES MYTH

Gantz, T. (1993) *Early Greek Myth: A guide to the literary and artistic sources*. Baltimore: 374–466.

Galinsky, K. (1972) *The Herakles Theme: The adaptations of the hero in literature from Homer to the twentieth century*. Oxford. An invaluable introduction to the widespread use of Hercules in literature.

Uhlenbrock, J. P. (ed.) (1986) *Herakles: Passage of the hero through 1000 years of classical art*. New Rochelle.

Notes

INTRODUCTION

David's Hercules and the Revolutionary Fête of August 1793: Hunt, L. (1984) *Politics, Culture, and Class in the French Revolution*. Berkeley: 94–114; Gutwirth, M. (1992) *The Twilight of the Goddesses: Women and representation in the French revolutionary era*. New Brunswick: 273–9; Roberts, W. (2000) *Jacques-Louis David and Jean-Louis Prieur, revolutionary artists: the public, the populace, and images of the French Revolution*. Albany: 269–311; and Ozouf, M. (1988) *Festivals and the French Revolution*. Cambridge, Mass.

On Hercules in France, see Jung, M.-R. (1966) *Hercule dans la littérature française du XVIᵉ siècle. De l'Hercule courtois a l'Hercule baroque*. Geneva.

Notes and Bibliography

Pliny on wall-painting: *Naturalis Historia* 35.118. On wall-painting generally: Ling, R. (1991) *Roman Painting.* Cambridge. The houses of Pompeii: Clarke, J. R. (1991) *The Houses of Roman Italy, 100 BC–AD 250.* Berkeley and Oxford; Wallace-Hadrill, A. (1994) *Houses and Society in Pompeii and Herculaneum.* Princeton; and Zanker, P. (1998) *Pompeii: Public and private life.* Revealing Antiquity 11, trans. Schneider, Cambridge, Mass.

The paintings in the House of the Vettii: Archer, W. A. (1981) *The Paintings of the Casa dei Vettii in Pompeii.* 2 vols., PhD dissertation, University of Virginia; Brilliant, R. (1986) *Visual Narratives: Storytelling in Etruscan and Roman art.* Ithaca, New York: 71–81; Clarke (1991): 208–35; Thompson, M. (1961) 'The Monumental and Literary Evidence for Programmatic Painting in Antiquity', *Marsyas* 9: 36–77; and Wirth, T. (1983) 'Zum Bildprogramm der Räume n and p in der Casa dei Vettii', *Mitteilungen des deutschen Archäologischen Instituts. Römische Abteilung* 90: 449–55. For Hercules in Pompeii, see Coralini, A. (2001) *Hercules domesticus: immagini di Ercole nelle case della regione vesuviana.* Naples. Hercules as founder of Pompeii: *Solinus* 2,5.

Hercules strangling snakes: Apollodorus, *Library* 2.4.8; Diodorus Siculus 4.10.1; Pindar, *Nemean Odes* 1.33–49; Theocritus, *Idylls* 24; and Virgil, *Aeneid* 8.288. For artistic representations: Brendel. O. (1932) 'Der schlangenwürgende Herakliskos', *Jahrbuch des deutschen archäologischen Instituts* 47: 191–238.

Hercules

Amphitryon and Alcmena: Apollodorus, *Library* 2.4.6–8;
and [Hesiod], *Shield of Heracles*, 1–26. The conception of
Hercules: Apollodorus, *Library* 2.4.8; Diodorus Siculus
4.9.1–4; and [Hesiod], *Shield of Heracles* 27–56. For dra-
matic interpretations: Costa, C. D. N. (1965) 'The
Amphitruo Theme' in T. A. Dorey and D. R. Dudley
(eds.) *Roman Drama*, New York: 87-122; Galinsky (1972):
81-100; Lindberger, O. (1956) *The Transformations of
Amphitryon*. Stockholm; Passage, C. E., and Mantinband,
J. E. (1974) *Amphitryon: The Legend and Three Plays in
New Verse Translations*. Chapel Hill; Kunze, M., Metzler,
D. and Riedel, V. (eds.) (1993) *Amphitryon: ein griechisches
Motiv in der europäischen Literatur und auf dem Theater*.
Hamburg; and Shero, L. R. (1956) 'Alcmena and
Amphitryon in ancient and modern drama', *Transactions of
the American Philological Association* 87: 192–238.

Plautus' *Amphitruo*: Christenson, D. M. (2000) *Plautus.
Amphitruo*. Cambridge; Galinsky, G. K. (1966) 'Scipionic
Themes in Plautus' *Amphitruo*', *Transactions of the American
Philological Association* 97: 203–35; and Prescott, H. W.
(1913) 'The *Amphitruo* of *Plautus'*, *Classical Philology* 8:
14–22. Shakespeare and Plautus: Schrader, W. (1993)
'Shakespeare und das Amphitryo-Motiv' in Kunze et al.
(1993): 32–40. The south Italian vase-painting with Zeus,
Hermes and Alcmene (Vatican U 19, inv. 17106):
Trendall, A. D. (1987) *The Red-Figured Vases of Paestum*.
London: 124–6, no. 176.

Rape in myth: Lefkowitz, M. R. (1993) 'Seduction and
Rape in Greek Myth' in A. E. Laiou (ed.) *Consent and*

Coercion to Sex and Marriage in Ancient and Medieval Societies.
Washington: 17–38; Robson, J. E. (1997) 'Bestiality and
bestial rape in Greek myth' in S. Deacy and K. F. Pierce
(eds.) *Rape in Antiquity*. London: 65–96; and Zeitlin, F.
(1986) 'Configurations of Rape in Greek Myth' in S.
Tomaselli and R. Porter (eds.) *Rape*. Oxford: 122–51.
Athenian attitudes to rape: Cohen, D. (1991) *Law,
Sexuality and Society: The enforcement of morals in classical
Athens*. Cambridge: 98–170; 'Consent and sexual relations
in classical Athens' in Laiou (1993): 5–16; and Harris, E.
M. 'Did the Athenians regard seduction as a worse crime
than rape?', *Classical Quarterly* 40 (1990): 370–77. Zeus as
a snake: Plutarch, *Alexander* 2.1–3.2. Christian criticism:
Clement of Alexandria, *Exhortation to the Greeks* 2.32–33.
Molière: Bierman, J. (1993) 'Social and ethical confusion in
Molière's *Amphitryon*' in Kunze et al. (1993): 41–51.
Kleist: Allen, S. (1996) *The Plays of Heinrich von Kleist. Ideals
and illusions*. Cambridge: 107–38; Bachmaier, H. and
Horst, T. (eds.) (1983) *Heinrich von Kleist: 'Amphitryon'.
Erläuterungen und Dokumente*. Stuttgart; Stahl, E. L. (1948)
Heinrich von Kleist's Dramas. Oxford; Stephens, A. (1994)
Heinrich von Kleist: The dramas and stories. Oxford;
Wittkowski, W. (1969) 'Der neue Prometheus: Kleists
Amphitryon zwischen Molière und Giradoux' in W.
Müller-Seidel (ed.) *Kleist und Frankreich*. Berlin: 27–82;
and (1978) *Heinrich von Kleists 'Amphitryon': Materialien
zur Rezeption und Interpretation*. Quellen und Forschungen
zur Sprach- und Kulturgeschichte der germanischen
Völker. Neue Folge, no. 72. Berlin and New York.

Hercules

Alcmena's pregnancy and the birth of Hercules: Diodorus
Siculus 4.9.4; Homer, *Iliad* 19.95–124; and Ovid,
Metamorphoses 9.280–323.
The suckling of Hercules by Hera: Diodorus Siculus 4.9.6;
and Eratosthenes, *Catasterismoi* 44.
The house of D. Octavius Quartio: Clarke (1991): 23–4,
193–207; Maiuri, A. (1947) *La casa di Loreio Tiburtino e la
villa di Diomede in Pompei.* Rome; and Zanker, P. (1979)
'Die Villa als Vorbild des späten pompeijanischen
Wohngeschmacks', *Jahrbuch des deutschen archäologischen
Instituts* 94: 460–523; (1998): 145–7. The statuette of
Hercules: Coralini (2001): 173–4. The garden statuary:
Jashemski, W. F. (1979–) *The Gardens of Pompeii,
Herculaneum and the Villas Destroyed by Vesuvius.* New
Rochelle: i.45, ii.78-83.
Influence of Euripides, *Bacchae*: Tomasello, E. (1958)
'Rappresentazione figurate del mito di Penteo', *Sicolorum
Gymnasium* 11: 219–41, 220–22. Dirce: Apollodorus,
Library 3.5.5; Hyginus, *Fabulae* 7 and 8; and Ovid,
Metamorphoses 6.110. Paintings of Dirce in Pompeii and
Herculaneum: Heger, F. 'Dirke', *LIMC* nos. 11–18.
Amphitryon releasing the snakes is recorded by Pherecydes:
Apollodorus, *Library* 2.4.8. The only other depiction of
the scene is now lost. For discussion and drawings:
Coralini (2001): 199–201.

CHAPTER TWO

Linus: Diodorus Siculus 3.67; Herodotus, *Histories* 2.79;

Pausanias 9.29.9 and Theocritus *Idylls* 29.103. The education of Hercules: Apollodorus, *Library* 2.4.9; and Theocritus *Idylls* 24.103–39.

Douris kylix (Munich 2646, Beazley, *ARV* 437.128): Buitron-Oliver, D. (1995) *Douris: A Master-Painter of Athenian Red-Figure Vases*, Mainz; Lissarague, F. (1987) *The Aesthetics of the Greek Banquet*, trans. A. Szegedy-Maszak, Princeton: 131. The symposium: Davidson, J. N. (1997) *Courtesans and Fishcakes: The consuming passions of classical Athens*. London; Murray, O. (ed.) (1990) *Sympotica: A symposium on the symposium*. Oxford.

The temple of Hercules and the Muses: Viscogliosi, A. 'Hercules Musarum, aedes', *LTUR* III.17–19. The 'Gallic Heracles': Lucian, *Heracles*. For the reception of this figure and his tremendous popularity in France: Galinsky (1972): 222–3 and Jung, M.-R. (1966) *Hercule dans la littérature française du XVI siècle*. Geneva: 73–93.

Activities as a cowherd: Apollodorus, *Library* 2.4.10–12; and Diodorus Siculus 4.10.3–5. Hercules and the daughters of Thespius: Athenaeus, *Deipnosophistae* 13.4; Apollodorus, *Library* 2.4.11; Diodorus Siculus 4.29.2–3; and Pausanias 9.27.6–7.

The 'Choice of Hercules': Xenophon, *Memorabilia* 2.1.21–34; Galinsky (1972): 101–25; Kuntz, M. (1984) 'The Prodikean "Choice of Herakles". A reshaping of myth', *The Classical Journal* 89: 163–81; McLachlan, J. (1974) 'The *Choice of Hercules*. American Student Societies in the early 19th century' in Kagan, R. L. et al. (eds.) *The University in Society*. 2 vols., Princeton: ii.449–94; and

Hercules

Panofsky, E. (1930) *Hercules am Scheidewege und andere antike Bildstoffe in der neueren Kunst*. Leipzig. Great Seal of the United States: Guggisberg, M. (2002) 'Herakles im Weißen Haus: Zu einer italischen Bronzestatuette John F. Kennedys', *Antike Welt* 33: 17–23; Schleiner, W. (1976) 'The Infant Hercules: Franklin's design for a medal commemorating American liberty', *Eighteenth-Century Studies* 10: 235-44; and Sommer, F. H. (1961) 'Emblem and Device: The Origin of the Great Seal of the United States', *Art Quarterly* 24: 57–76, 65–67. Dinner service, Baca, A. R. (1996) *Napoleon, Russia, and the Olympian Gods: The Olympic Service of the Armory Museum in the Kremlin*. Hollywood: 20. Purpose behind Hercules' conception: Diodorus Siculus 4.9.3, and [Hesiod], *Shield of Heracles*, 27–9. Allegorical interpretations of the Hercules myths: Galinsky (1972): 56.

Camerino Farnese: Martin, J. R. (1965) *The Farnese Gallery*, Princeton: 21–35. The *Judgement of Hercules* is currently held in the Pinacoteca Nationale, Naples. See also Marzik, I. (1986) *Das Bildprogramm der Galleria Farnese in Rom*, Berlin for the continuation of the classicising programme into the main gallery.

Hercules being punished by Athena: Le Gros, W. B. (1835) *Fables and tales, suggested by the frescos of Pompeii and Herculaneum*. London: 175–85.

Cicero's opinion on the 'Choice of Hercules': Cicero, *De officiis* 3.5.25.

CHAPTER THREE

Caesar as Hercules: Heywood, Thomas (1612, repr. 1973) *An Apology for Actors*: E3ᵛ.

Canova: Adams, R. M. (1974) *The Roman Stamp: Frame and façade in some forms of Neo-Classicism*. Berkeley and London: 163–83; Albrizzi, I. (1876) *The Works of Antonio Canova*. London; Apolloni, M. F. (1992) *Canova*, Florence; Bassi, E. (1957) *Antonio Canova*. Milan; D'Este, A. (1864) *Memorie di Antonio Canova*. Florence; Honour, H. (1968) *Neo-Classicism*. Harmondsworth; Quatremère de Quincy, A. C. (1834) *Canova et ses ouvrages*. Paris; and Licht, F. (1983) *Canova*. New York. Eros and Thantaos: Stefani, O. (1992) *Canova pittore*. Milan.

Canova's preliminary sketches on the exploits of Hercules: Bassi, E. (1959) *Il Museo Civico di Bassano*. Venice: esp. E.b.171.1182, F.2.15.1430, F.2.29.1444, F.3.57.1566, and F.6.31.1680.

Hercules and Lichas: Sophocles, *The Women of Trachis*; Ovid, *Metamorphoses* 9.155, 211; Hyginus, *Fabulae* 36; Strabo, *Geography*, 10.1.9.

Casts and models in Possagno: Bassi, E. (1957) *La Gipsoteca di Possagno*. Venice: nos. 137–9; Stefani (1992): 60–64, Licht (1983): 262-66. Engravings of the reliefs: Pezzini, G. and Fiorani, F. (1993) *Canova e l'incisione*. Venice: no. 34.

Dispute with Egrinus: Apollodorus, *Library* 2.4.11; Diodorus Siculus 4.10.3–5 and Pausanias 9.37.3. Theseus: Brommer, F. (1982) *Theseus*. Darmstadt; Calame, C.

(1990) *Thésée et l'imaginaire athénien*. Lausanne; and Neils, J. (1987) *The Youthful Deeds of Theseus*. Rome.

Euripides: There is a convenient translation by R. Waterfield of Euripides' *Herakles* in the Oxford World Classics series (2003). Text and commentary: Barlow, S. A. (1998) *Euripides' Heracles*, rev. ed., Warminster. Hercules in Greek tragedy: Ehrenberg, V. (1946) 'Tragic Herakles' in *Aspects of the Ancient World*, Oxford; Silk. M. S. (1985) 'Heracles and Greek Tragedy', *Greece and Rome* 32: 1–22. Subsequent reception: Riley, K. (2004) 'Reasoning Madness: The Reception and Performance of Euripides' *Herakles*. D.Phil. dissertation The University of Oxford. Phyrnichus: Herodotus, *Histories* 6.21. Lycus and Amphitryon: Euripides, *Heracles* 140–69 (Lycus) and 170–235 (Amphitryon).

Hera: Kerényi, K. (1972) *Zeus und Hera: Urbild des Vaters, des Gatten und der Frau*. Leiden; and Pötscher, W. (1987) *Hera; Eine Strukturanalyse im Vergleich mit Athena*. Darmstadt. Sanctuary at Samos: Herodotus, *Histories* 3.60. Statues of Hera: Pausanias 2.17.3–4. Hera's blessing: Herodotus, *Histories* 1.31.

Conception of Hephaestus: Apollodorus, *Library* 1.3.5; Homer, *Iliad* 1.590, 18.394; Hyginus, *Fabulae* 166; Virgil, *Eclogues* 4.62.

Bellerophon: Apollodorus, *Library* 2.3.1; Hyginus, *Fabulae* 157; and Pindar, *Isthmian Odes* 7.44. Ixion: Apollodorus, *Library* 1.8.2; Diodorus Siculus 4.69; Hyginus, *Fabulae* 14; and Pindar, *Pythian Odes* 2.39. Marsyas: Apollodorus, *Library* 1.4.2, Diodorus Siculus 3.58 and Hyginus, *Fabulae* 165.

Notes and Bibliography

Arachne: Ovid, *Metamorphoses* 6.1–145; and Virgil, *Georgics* 4.246.

Seneca: Griffin, M. T. (1975) *Seneca: A philosopher in politics.* Oxford. Seneca's *Hercules Furens* is translated by J. G. Fitch in the Loeb library edition of the writing of Seneca. He has also produced a valuable commentary on the text: Fitch, J. G. (1987) *Seneca's Hercules Furens. A critical text with introduction and commentary*, Ithaca and London. cf. Shelton, J. A. (1978) *Seneca's Hercules Furens: Theme, structure, and style*, Göttingen. Hercules in Seneca's work: *De Beneficiis*, 1.13.1–3, 7.3.1; *Letters* 9.64; Galinsky (1972): 167–84. On the contrast between Hercules' labours and the actions of Cato: *De Constantia Sapientis* 2.1–2. Suicide of Seneca: Tacitus, *Annals* 15.60–63. Attitudes to suicide: Garrison, E. P. (1995) *Groaning Tears: Ethical and dramatic aspects of suicide in Greek tragedy*, Leiden; van Hoff, A. J. L. (1990) *From Autothanasia to Suicide: Self-killing in antiquity*, London; and James, C. (1969) "Whether 'tis nobler . . ." Some thoughts on the fate of Sophocles' Ajax and Euripides' Heracles, with special reference to the question of suicide, *Pegasus* 12: 10–20; *On the Brevity of Life* 7.4.

Jacopo Melani's opera, *Ercole in Tebe* (1661): Damerini, A. (1917) 'La partitura dell' *Ercole in Tebe* di Jacopo Melani con appendice sui musicisti fratelli di Jacopo', *Bollettino storico pistoiese* 19: 45; Weaver, R. L. and Weaver, N. W. (1978) *A Chronology of Florentine Theater 1590–1750*. Detroit.

Influence of Senecan drama in the Renaissance: Braden, G. (1985) *Renaissance Tragedy and the Senecan Tradition,*

New Haven and London; and Hunter, G. K. (1974) 'Seneca and English Tragedy' in C. D. N. Costa (ed.) *Seneca*, London: 166–204. Stage tradition of Hercules' madness in the Elizabethan period: Soellner, R. (1958) 'The madness of Herakles and the Elizabethans', *Comparative Literature* 10: 309–24. Diagnoses of Hercules' madness: Pseudo-Aristotle, *Problems* 30 953a; Nicholas of Damascus in *FGrH* 90 F 13.

CHAPTER FOUR

Murder and pollution: Parker, R. (1983) *Miasma: Pollution and purification in early Greek religion*. Oxford: 104–43; Johnston, S. I. (1999) *Restless Dead: Encounters between the Living and the Dead in Ancient Greece*. Berkeley and Los Angeles: 127–60. The purification of Hercules: Parker (1983): 381.

Trials of inanimate objects: Aeschines 3.244; Demosthenes 23.76; Pausanias 5.27.10, 6.11.6. MacDowell, D. M. (1963) *Athenian Homicide Law in the Age of the Orators*. Manchester: 85–9. Athenian murder trials in the open air: Antiphon 5.11.

Consultation of the Pythia: Apollodorus 2.4.12. Oracles, especially the Delphic oracle: Fontenrose, J. (1978) *The Delphic Oracle: Its responses and operations*. Berkeley and Los Angeles; Gould, J. (1985) 'On making sense of Greek religion' in P. Easterling and J. V. Muir (eds.) *Greek Religion and Society*. Cambridge: 1–33. Despondency at performing labours: Diodorus Siculus 4.11.1–2.

Notes and Bibliography

Eurystheus: Apollodorus, *Library* 2.45; Diodorus Siculus
4.9.4.

The Temple of Zeus at Olympia: Ashmole, B. and Yalouris,
N. (1967) *Olympia: The sculptures of the temple of Zeus.*
London; Osborne, R. (1998) *Archaic and Classical Art.*
Oxford: 169–74; Spivey, N. (1997) *Greek Art.* London:
217–24. Reconstruction of the metopes: Stucchi, S.
(1952–4) 'La decorazione figurata del Tempio di Zeus ad
Olimpia', *Annuario della Scuola Archeologica di Atene,*
30–32: 23–129. Pausanias' description of the metopes:
Pausanias 5.10.9.

Foundation of the Olympic Games: Diodorus Siculus 4.14;
Pindar, *Olympic Odes* 10.55–9.

Viewing architectural sculpture: Osborne, R. G. (1987) 'The
viewing and obscuring of the Parthenon frieze', *Journal of
Hellenic Studies* 107: 98–105.

Treasury of the Athenians at Delphi: Audiat, J. (1933) *Le
trésor des Athéniens.* Fouilles de Delphes 2, Paris. Cycnus:
[Hesiod], *The Shield of Heracles*; Vian, E. (1945) 'Le
Combat d'Héraklès et de Kyknos d'après les documents
figurés du VIe siècle', *Revue des Études Anciennes* 47: 5–32.

Pelops and Oinomaus: Pindar, *Olympian Odes* 1.67–90;
Apollodorus, *Epitome* 2.4–9; Pausanias 5.1.6–7, 2.18.2,
8.14.11; Diodorus Siculus 4.73; Kyrieleis, H. (1997)
'Zeus and Pelops in the East Pediment of the Parthenon'
in D. Buitron-Oliver (ed.) *The Interpretation of Architectural
Sculpture in Greece and Rome*, New Haven: 13–28. Atreus
and Thyestes: Seneca, *Thyestes.*

The battle between Lapiths and centaurs: Ovid,

Metamorphoses 12.210–535; Padgett, J. M. (2003) 'Horse Men: Centaurs and Satyrs in Early Greek Art' in Padgett, J. M. (ed.) *The Centaur's Smile: The human animal in Greek art*. New Haven: 3–48; Osborne, R. (1994) 'Framing the centaur: reading fifth-century architectural sculpture' in S. Goldhill and R. Osborne (eds.) *Art and Text in Ancient Greek Culture*. Cambridge: 52–84. Hercules and the Lapiths: Apollodorus, *Library* 2.7.7.

The Nemean lion: Apollodorus, *Library* 2.5.1; Bacchylides, *Victory Odes* 9.6–9; Diodorus Siculus 4.10; Hesiod, *Theogony* 327–9. Athletes wrestling with lions: Pausanias 6.5.5.

The hydra: Apollodorus, *Library* 2.5.2; Pausanias 2.37.4. Envenoming of arrows, see Mayor, A. (2004) *Greek Fire, Poison Arrows and Scorpion Bombs: Biological and chemical weapons in the ancient world*. London.

Cerynitian hind: Apollodorus, *Library* 2.5.3; Pindar, *Olympian Odes* 3.28–34; Diodorus Siculus 4.13.1. Acteon: Ovid, *Metamorphoses* 3.131–252.

Chrion and Pholos: Apollodorus, *Library* 2.5.4; Diodorus Siculus 4.12; Euripides, *Heracles* 364–75; Philostratus, *Imagines* 2.2; Theocritus *Idylls* 154–7. River Anigrus: Pausanias 5.5.10.

Augean stables: Apollodorus, *Library* 2.5.5; Diodorus Siculus 4.13.3, Pausanias 5.1.9–10.

Stymphalian birds: Apollodorus, *Library* 2.5.6; Apollonius of Rhodes, *Argonautica* 2.1052–7; Diodorus Siculus 4.13.2; Pausanias 8.22.4–5.

Richelieu: Goldfarb, H. T. (ed.) *Richelieu: Art and Power*.

Montreal, esp. 127–36, 240–42, 282–3, 305–7; Menard, J. (1985) 'Richlieu et le théâtre' in *Richelieu et le monde d'e-spirit*. Paris: 193–206. Poussin and the Grande Gallerie du Louvre: Van Helsdingen, H. W. (1971) 'Notes on Two Sheets of Sketches by Nicolas Poussin for the Long Gallery of the Louvre', *Simiolus* 5: 172–84; Rosenberg, P. and Prat, L.-A. (1994) *Nicolas Poussin, 1594–1665: Catalogue raisonné des dessins*. 2 vols., Milan: i.414–26. Vignon: Mignot, C. (1998) 'L'*Hercules admirandus* de Richelieu' in C. Mignot and P. P. Bassani (eds.) *Claude Vignon en son temps*. Tours: 21–5; Bassani, P. P. (1992) *Claude Vignon, 1593–1670*. Paris: 276–8.

CHAPTER FIVE

Alexander: Arrian, *Anabasis of Alexander* 5.26.5–6. Images of Alexander: Stewart, A. (1993) *Faces of Power: Alexander's image and Hellenistic politics*. Berkeley and Los Angeles.

Cimon and the bones of Theseus: Plutarch, *Cimon* 8.5–6. Orestes' bones: Herodotus, *Histories* 1.66–8; Pausanias 3.3.5–6, 3.11.10, 8.54.4. Fossilised bones: Mayor, A. (2000) *The First Fossil Hunters: Paleontology in Greek and Roman times*. Princeton: 104–56.

Cretan bull: Apollodorus, *Library* 2.5.7; Diodorus Siculus 4.13.4; Pausanias 1.27.9–10. Europa: Ovid, *Metamorphoses* 2.836–75. Daedalus: Apollodorus, *Library* 3.5.8; Diodorus Siculus 4.76–9; Ovid, *Metamorphoses* 8.152–235; Frontisi-Ducroux, F. (1975) *Dédale, mythologie de l'artisan en Grèce ancienne*. Paris.

Hercules

Mares of Diomedes: Apollodorus, *Library* 2.5.8; Diodorus
Siculus 4.15.3–4; Euripides, *Herakles* 379–85; Philostratus,
Imagines 2.25. Mares' milk: Herodotus, *Histories* 4.2. Freud
and the Medusa: Garber, M. and Vickers, N. (2000) *The
Medusa Reader*. London. Gender: Loraux, N. (1990)
'Herakles: the super-male and the feminine' in D. M.
Halperin, J. Winkler, and F. Zeitlin (eds.) *Before Sexuality:
The construction of erotic experience in the ancient Greek world.*
Princeton: 21–52.

The belt of Hippolyta: Apollodorus, *Library* 2.5.8;
Apollonius of Rhodes, *Argonautica* 774–9; Diodorus
Siculus 4.16; Euripides, *Heracles* 409–18. Amazons: von
Bothmer, D. (1957) *Amazons in Greek Art*. Oxford;
Harrison, E. B. (1966) 'The composition of the
Amazonomachy on the shield of Athena Parthenos',
Hesperia 35: 107–33; Henderson, J. (1994) 'Timeo
Danaos: Amazons in early Greek art and pottery' in S.
Goldhill and R. Osborne (eds.) *Art and Text in Ancient
Greek Culture*. Cambridge: 85–137. Funeral orations:
Loraux, N. (1986) *The Invention of Athens: The funeral ora-
tion in the classical city*. Harvard.

Hercules at Troy: Apollodorus, *Library* 2.5.9; Diodorus
Siculus 4.42; Ovid, *Metamorphoses* 11.215–219.

Cattle of Geryon: Apollodorus, *Library* 2.5.10; Diodorus
Siculus 4.17–18; Hesiod, *Theogony* 287–94; Pausanias
4.36.3. Snake woman: Herodotus, *Histories* 4.8–10.
Hermes: *Homeric Hymn to Hermes*. Trip in the cup of the
sun: Athenaeus 11.469.d, 470 c–d. Drink and sea-sick-
ness: Timaeus *FGrH* 566 F149; Davies, M. (1978)

'Sailing, Rowing and Sporting in One's Cup on the Wine Dark Sea' in *Athens Comes of Age: From Solon to Salamis*. Princeton: 72–90. Cacus: Diodorus Siculus 4.20–22; Ovid, *Fasti* 1.543–78; Virgil, *Aeneid* 8.184–279. Italy: Dionysius of Halicarnassus, *Roman Antiquities* 34–5, 39–44; Propertius 4.9; Galinsky (1972): 126–52.

Apples of the Hesperides: Apollodorus, *Library* 2.5.11; Apollonius of Rhodes, *Argonautica* 1397–1405; Diodorus Siculus 4.26; Euripides, *Herakles* 394–9; Hesiod, *Theogony* 215–16; Pausanias 5.18.4.

Proteus: Homer, *Odyssey* 4.354–570. Antaeus: Apollodorus, *Library* 2.5.11; Diodorus Siculus 4.17; Ovid, *Metamorphoses* 9.182–3; Pindar, *Isthmian Odes* 4.52–60. Busiris: Apollodorus, *Library* 2.5.11; Diodorus Siculus 4.18, 27.

Automata: Hero, *Pneumatica* 1.41; Brumbaugh, R. S. (1966) *Ancient Greek Gadgets and Machines*. New York.

Hercules and Cerberus: Apollodorus, *Library* 2.5.12; Bacchylides, *Victory Odes* 5.56–175; Diodorus Siculus 4.25.1; Euripides, *Herakles* 425–8. Aconite: Theophrastus, *On Plants* 9.16.4–7. Alcestis: Euripides, *Alcestis*. Katabasis: Clark, R. J. (1979) *Catabasis: Vergil and the Wisdom Tradition*. Amsterdam. Curses: Gager, J. G. (ed.) (1992) *Curse Tablets and Binding Spells from the Ancient World*. Oxford. Sites of descent: Ogden, D. (2001) *Greek and Roman Necromancy*. Princeton: 29–42.

CHAPTER SIX

Hercules and Apollo: Apollodorus, *Library* 2.6.2. Amphitryon and the vixen: Apollodorus, *Library* 2.4.6–7. Corax and Tisias: Aristotle, *Art of Rhetoric* 1402a18–21; Plato, *Phaedrus* 273a–b; Sextus Empiricus, *Against the Professors* 2.96–9. Tripods: Amandry, P. (1976) 'Trépieds d'Athènes: I. Dionysies, *Bulletin de correspondance hellénique* 100: 15–93; Wilson, P. (2000) *The Athenian Institution of the Khoregia: The chorus, the city and the stage.* Cambridge: 199–213, 219–25, 303. Iole: 2.6.1–2. Hierosulia: Cohen, D. (1983) *Theft in Athenian Law.* Munich: 93–111; Todd, S. C. (1993) *The Shape of Athenian Law.* Cambridge: 307–10. Aesop in Delphi: *Life of Aesop* 124–47. Sacred Wars: Davies, J. (1994) 'The tradition about the First Sacred War' in S. Hornblower (ed.) *Greek Historiography.* Oxford: 193–213. Philip of Macedon: Hammond, N. G. L. (1994) *Philip of Macedon.* Baltimore: 45–52, 90–97.

Hercules and Omphale: Apollodorus, *Library* 2.6.3; Diodorus Siculus 4.31.5–8; Ovid, *Heroides* 55–86. Red-figure vase: BM E370; cf. Carawan, E. (2000) 'Deianeira's guilt', *Transactions of the American Philological Association* 130: 189–237. Rubens: Belkin, K. L. (1998) *Rubens.* London; Foucart, J. (1985) 'Les retrouvailles d'un grand Rubens du Louvre', *La revue du Louvre et des musées de France* 5–6: 387–96; Huemer, F. (1979) 'A Dionysiac connection in an early Rubens', *Art Bulletin* 61.4: 562–74; Stechow, W. (1968) *Rubens and the Classical Tradition.* Cambridge. Belvedere torso: Bober, P. P. and Rubinstein, H. (1986)

Renaissance Artists and Antique Sculpture: A handbook of sources. Oxford: 166–8. Queen Christina: Baudoin, F. (1966) 'Deux tableaux de Rubens de la collection de la Reine Christine: "Hercule et Omphale" et "La mort d'Adonis" in von Platen, M. (ed.) *Queen Christina of Sweden: Sources and documents*. Stockholm: 16–32; Biermann, V. (2001) 'The Virtue of a King and the Desire of a Woman? Mythological representations in the collection of Queen Christina' in M. Camille and A. Rifkin (eds.) *Other Objects of Desire: collectors and collecting queerly*. Oxford. Coypel and Boucher: Bailey, C. B. (1992) *The Loves of the Gods: Mythological painting from Watteau to David*. New York: 308–15, 372–9; Sheriff, M. D. (1998) 'Reading Jupiter Otherwise: Or Ovid's women in eighteenth-century art' in F. Van Keuren (ed.) *Myth, Sexuality and Power: Images of Jupiter in Western Art*. Providence; Vidal, M. (1992) *Watteau's Painted Conversations*. New Haven; de Vitis, M. (2002) *The Metamorphosis of Hercules: Journey of the hero through the art of the Ancien régime*. Unpublished dissertation, University of Sydney.

The Cercopes and Syleus: Apollodorus, *Library* 2.6.3–2.7.1; Diodorus Siculus 4.31.7. Trojan War: Apollodorus, *Library* 2.6.4; Diodorus Siculus 4.32.1–5. Augeas: Apollodorus, *Library* 2.7.2; Diodorus Siculus 4.33.1. Hylas: Apollonius of Rhodes, *Argonautica* 1.1207–1272; Clement of Alexandria, *Exhortation to the Greeks* 2.28; Theocritus, *Idylls* 13; Beye, C. R. (1982) *Epic and Romance in the 'Argonautica' of Apollonius*. Carbondale: 30, 93–5.

Hercules and Deianeira: Apollodorus, *Library* 2. 7.5–7;

Diodorus Siculus 4.35.1–36.5; Ovid, *Heroides* 9;
Sophocles, *Trachiniae*. Tragedy: Easterling, P. E. (1968)
'Sophocles, Trachiniae', *Bulletin of the Institute of Classical
Studies* 16: 58–69; Levett, B. (2004) *Sophocles: Women of
Trachis*. London; McCall, M. (1972) 'The *Trachiniae*:
Structure, Focus and Heracles', *American Journal of
Philology* 93: 142–63. Cicero translation: *Tusculans* 2.8.
Heroides: Anderson, W. S. (1973) 'The Heroides' in
Binns, J. W. (ed.) *Ovid*. London: 49–83; Jacobson, H.
(1974) *Ovid's Heroides*. Princeton; Verducci, F. (1985)
Ovid's Toyshop of the Heart: Epistulae Heroidum. Princeton;
Wilkinson, L. P. *Ovid Surveyed*. Cambridge.

Death and Apotheosis: Apollodorus, *Library* 2.7.7; Diodorus
Siculus 4.38–9; Lucian, *Dialogues of the Dead* 16. Christian
Hercules: Galinsky (1972): 202–6.

EPILOGUE

Children of Hercules: Apollodorus, *Library* 2.7.8; Euripides,
Children of Herakles; Isocrates, *Panegyric* 15; Lysias 2.11–16.
Telephus: Apollodorus, *Library* 2.7.4; Diodorus Siculus
4.33.7–12.

Hercules and bodybuilding: Wyke, M. (1997) 'Herculean
Muscle!: The Classicizing rhetoric of bodybuilding', *Arion*
4.3: 51–79. Sandow: Dutton, K. R. (1995) *The Perfectible
Body: The western ideal of physical development*. London:
119–29. Kasson, J. F. (2001) *Houdini, Tarzan, and the
Perfect Man: The white male body and the challenge of modernity in America*. New York: 21–76; Sandow, E. (1897)

Strength and How to Obtain It. London; Webster, D. (1979) *Barbells and Beefcake.* Irvine: 29–35.

Peplum cinema: Blanshard, A. J. L. and Shahabudin, K. (2003) 'Hercules – the Movie Star', *Omnibus* 45: 4–6; Lagny, M. (1992) 'Popular taste: The peplum' in R. Dyer and G. Vincendeau (eds.) *Popular European Cinema*, London: 163–80; Solomon, J. (2001) *The Ancient World in the Cinema.* New Haven: 119–22; Wyke (1997): 63–8. Levine's publicity campaign: Chapman, D. (2002) *Retro Stud: Muscle movie posters from around the world.* Portland: 7–13; Luciano, P. (1994) *With Fire and Sword: Italian spectacles on American Screens 1858–1968.* London: 12–13; Solomon (2001): 120. Schwarzenegger: Flynn, J. L. (1993) *The Films of Arnold Schwarzenegger.* New York: 18; Schwarzenegger, A. (1979) *Arnold: the Education of a Bodybuilder.* London: 63.

Disney's *Hercules*: Solomon (2001): 123–4; Thomas, B. (1992) *Disney's Art of Animation from Mickey Mouse to Hercules.* New York: 164–219.

Southern Italian column crater: Metropolitan Museum of Modern Art, inv. no. 50.11.4. Hercules and Daedalus: Apollodorus, *Library* 2.6.3.

Illustrations Credits

Illustration Credits

Index

Page numbers in *italics* refer to illustrations

Index

Index

Index

USA
  civil war cartoon, *114*
  seal, 33

Versailles, Palace of, 146
Vettius Conviva, Aulus, 3, 4
Vettius Restitutus, Aulus, 3, 4
Vignon, Claude, 85–8
violence
  classical interest in, 58–9
  and Hercules' labours, 60–1, 74,
    88
Voltaire, 12

Waterhouse, John William, 135
The Women of Trachis (Sophocles),
    57
wrestling, 76–7

Xenophanes, 167
xenophobia, 99–101, 106–7
Xenophon, 32–3

Zethus, 22
Zeus *see* Jupiter
Ziegfeld, Florenz, 156